INCLUDES 1 MAP!!!

D0051279

National Atomic Testing Museum **14**

EAST

FLAMINGO ROAD

EAST

ROAD

FLAMINGO

PARADISE

TROPICANA

AVE

EAST

AVENUE

TROPICANA

LAS

Harrah's/ The LINQ

Flamingo/ Caesars Palace

Paris Las Vegas **17**

Bally's/ Paris

Miracle Mile Shops **18**

Planet Hollywood **18**

MGM Grand

MGM Grand **11**

The LINQ & High Roller **8**

The Forum Shops **2**

Bellagio **1**

The Cosmopolitan of Las Vegas **4**

CityCenter **3**

BOULEVARD

VEGAS

New York New York **16**

Luxor **9**

Shark Reef **20**

# Fodor's
## 25 Best

# LAS VEGAS

# Contents

## KEY TO SYMBOLS

| | |
|---|---|
| ✚ Map reference to the accompanying pull-out map | 🍴 Restaurant or café |
| ✉ Address | 🚇 Nearest monorail station |
| ☎ Telephone number | 🚌 Nearest bus route |
| ⏱ Opening/closing times | ♿ Facilities for visitors with disabilities |

## ENTERTAINMENT 124

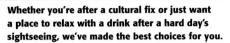

Whether you're after a cultural fix or just want a place to relax with a drink after a hard day's sightseeing, we've made the best choices for you.

## EAT 136

Uncover great dining experiences, from a quick bite at lunch to top-notch evening meals.

## SLEEP 150

We've brought together the best hotels in the city, whatever budget you're on.

## NEED TO KNOW 160

The practical information you need to make your trip run smoothly.

## PULL-OUT MAP

The pull-out map with this book is a comprehensive street plan of the city. We've given grid references within the book for each sight and listing.

| | |
|---|---|
| 🛈 Tourist information | 🖐 Admission charges: |
| 🔢 Other practical information | Very expensive (over $50), |
| ▷ Further information | Expensive ($21–$50), |
| | Moderate ($7–$20) and |
| | Inexpensive (under $7) |

# Introducing Las Vegas

Las Vegas is the entertainment capital of the world, where sleep is a mere inconvenience interrupting a continuous stream of fun, and where everything is bigger, louder, flashier and trashier than anywhere else in the world.

From the moment you cruise into town it will strike you that this is like no other place. The scale of everything is overwhelming, and The Strip (Las Vegas Boulevard South) in all its blazing glory is a thing of wonderment. Where else can you capture a skyscape that includes the Eiffel Tower, St. Mark's Campanile, an Egyptian pyramid and the Statue of Liberty on the same street? Prepare yourself for a fantasy world made real, where volcanoes erupt and Roman statues come alive.

Evolving from the early saloons, the first casinos and hotels were built in the Downtown area in the 1930s, followed by the expansion of The Strip in the 1940s. Since the late 1980s, mega-hotels have emerged—combining casinos, shopping malls, restaurants, spas and theaters—to offer the complete experience for gamers and vacationers alike. So what continues to bring millions of visitors here annually—gambling millions of dollars in the process? Las Vegas is an ever-evolving metropolis with a restless spirit that is part of its eclectic appeal. Hotels are regularly torn down to make way for brand-new ideas, and entertainment programs constantly change. Vegas is now home to some of the top restaurants in the world, many run by celebrity chefs, and most of the big names in designer fashion have made their mark on the shopping scene.

You might be forgiven for believing Las Vegas is not synonymous with culture and outdoor adventure, but beyond the neon there are some great museums and galleries, and ballet, jazz, symphony orchestras and opera blend perfectly. Away from the man-made wonders are dramatic canyons, dams and sparkling lakes, and the terrain lends itself to some of the finest golf courses. But no matter how you spend your time here, this crazy city will never let you forget that the driving force is gambling.

## FACTS AND FIGURES

- There are more than 15,000 miles (24,100km) of neon tubing in The Strip and Downtown Las Vegas.
- There are around 315 weddings per day in Vegas.
- There are around 200,000 slot machines to take your cash.
- On average, each visitor to Las Vegas spends US$445 on gambling.

## RAT PACK MEETS VEGAS

In the 1960s, Las Vegas was dominated by a group of singing and acting stars. Frank Sinatra first performed at the Sands Hotel in 1960, with John F. Kennedy in the audience. Thereafter, Sinatra, along with Dean Martin, Sammy Davis Jr., Peter Lawford and Joey Bishop—collectively known as the Rat Pack—dominated the scene and drew in huge crowds.

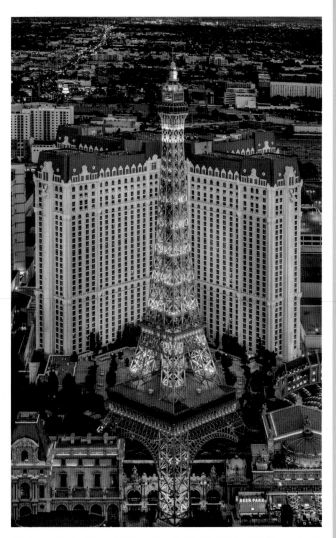

## TYING THE KNOT IN STYLE

Thousands of people are following in the footsteps of the rich and famous and saying "I do" in Vegas. Famous couples such as Elvis and Priscilla Presley, and Bruce Willis and Demi Moore, have been joined by Mr. and Mrs. Average from countries as far apart as Britain and Japan, to get married in some of the 50 or so wedding chapels (▷ 60–61).

## HOW IT BEGAN

Spawned from a trading post along the old Spanish Trail, Las Vegas became a popular stop for its freshwater spring. The prospect of gold added to the lure and later the building of the Hoover Dam secured the city's future. The liberal state laws of Nevada allowed the growth of the casinos, and soon the little campsite in the desert developed into a city.

# Focus On Playing the Game

Whether you're hoping to hit the jackpot on the high-stakes tables, or just fancy a taste of the slots, it's worth finding out first what the main games are and picking up a few tips along the way.

### The Games

**Baccarat** Two-card game, largely based on luck, with the aim of getting a hand adding up to a maximum of nine points, known as a "natural." One player at a time takes on the bank. It is often given a sophisticated image, with dealers dressed in tuxedos, and played at a table away from the rest of the casino. Best places to play are Monte Carlo, MGM Grand, Aria, Wynn, Bellagio, The Venetian.

**Blackjack** Card game, one of the many variations of Pontoon, or 21. Played at a special semicircular table, with up to seven players competing against the dealer. Best places to play are The Mirage, Caesars Palace, Flamingo, El Cortez, Orleans, Palms.

**Craps** Fast, exciting and one of the most popular games, with one player at a time rolling two dice at a special table, holding as many as 16 players, and controlled by a "boxman," who stands between the two dealers and monitors the play. To win at craps, the ultimate aim is to roll a seven. Best place to play is Casino Royale (opposite The Mirage).

**Keno** Similar to bingo, it originated in China. It's a very popular, easy and informal game, but with odds heavily stacked in favor of the house. Best places to play are Flamingo, Orleans, Bally's, Treasure Island.

**Pai Gow** Two-handed poker, based on an original Chinese domino game, with six players taking on the banker. Best places to play are Gold Coast, Orleans, The LINQ.

**Roulette** Possibly the most famous casino game, betting on a little ball landing in a numbered slot in a spinning wheel. It is played with special chips, with each player having a

*Las Vegas is not called the entertainment capital of the world for nothing. Nevada law permits a wide variety of gaming, including traditional card and dice table*

different color. If you win and want to cash in your winnings, the dealer will exchange these for winning chips, which you take to a casino cashier. Best places to play are MGM Grand, Aria, Bellagio, Mandalay Bay, El Cortez.

**Slots** These are highly sophisticated computerized machines, paying jackpots of up to $10,000 or more. Serious players guard their machines jealously—if you're playing for hours and need a food or toilet break, ask an attendant to look after your slot for you (a tip is expected). Best places to play are Slots A Fun (2890 Las Vegas Boulevard South, beside Circus Circus), Palms, Gold Coast.

**Texas Hold 'em** Five-card game against the dealer, and currently the most popular form of poker with betting limits from $1 to $25,000 or more. Best places to play are The Venetian, Bellagio , Rio, Golden Nugget.

**Video Poker** Extremely popular and fast version of the classic card game. It is played at a machine and is great if you don't want to sit down with experienced poker players. Best places to play are Palms, South Point.

### Lessons

Free daytime lessons in craps, roulette and blackjack are offered at many casinos. Dealers often give advice during live games. The Stratosphere and Excalibur offer poker lessons.

### Do's and Don'ts

● Choose which game to play and learn the rules first.
● Set a limit on how much you're going to spend before you start playing, and stick to it.
● Check if drinks offered by the cocktail servers are free—they often are if you're playing, but don't forget to tip.
● Keep your money in your sight and reach at all times.
● By law, players have to be 21 or older to gamble in Las Vegas casinos.

*games, slot machines of virtually every type, race and sports books, high-tech electronic gambling devices and international games of chance*

# Top Tips For...

These great suggestions will help you tailor your ideal visit to Las Vegas, no matter how you choose to spend your time.

### Something for Free
You can't help but be drawn to the **Bellagio Fountains** (▷ 14–15).
Take a trip downtown to see the **Fremont Street Experience** (▷ 24–25), a dazzling display of images cast on an LED-light roof.
Visit one of the free, live animal attractions, such as **The Wildlife Habitat** at the Flamingo (▷ 74).

### Getting the Heart Pumping
Great for an adrenaline rush, brave the thrill rides at the **Stratosphere Tower** (▷ 56–57).
The **Big Apple Coaster** at New York New York (▷ 44–45) is an exhilarating experience.
Take to the sky in a helicopter or small plane for a bird's-eye view of the **Hoover Dam** (▷ 26–27).

### Hitting the Shopping Malls
At the **Fashion Show** (▷ 68) mall you'll find the leading US department stores and more.
For a true smorgasbord of shopping deals, head for one of the outlet malls, such as **Las Vegas North Premium Outlets** (▷ 120).
Entertainment and retail therapy go hand-in-hand at **Miracle Mile Shops** (▷ 48–49).
Sample unique shopping under an artificial sky at **The Forum Shops** (▷ 16–17).
You will almost believe you are in Venice at the **Grand Canal Shoppes** (▷ 119).

### Being Pampered
Travel from the airport to your hotel in a **stretch limousine** (▷ 167).
Check in at one of the most luxurious resorts, such as the **Bellagio** (▷ 14–15).
Indulge yourself in ultimate pampering at **Qua Baths & Spa** at Caesars Palace (▷ 72).

*Clockwise from top: The Bellagio's spectacular dancing fountains; Caesars Palace at dusk; the lobby at Planet Hollywood; step into relaxation at Qua Baths & Spa;*

### Delectable Hot Spots

Dine in restaurants created by celebrity chefs—try **Jaleo** (▷ 144) at The Cosmopolitan, **Michael Mina** (▷ 145) at Bellagio and Thomas Keller's **Bouchon** (▷ 141) at The Venetian.

Take advantage of some of the city's finest French cuisine; **Joël Robuchon** at the MGM Grand (▷ 144) is one of the best.

Enjoy the Bellagio's fountain show from **Mon Ami Gabi** (▷ 145) at Paris Las Vegas.

For a sweet finish to your culinary tour, have dessert at **Jean Philippe Patisserie** inside Aria, CityCenter (▷ 144).

### High-Energy Clubs

Show your moves on the dance floor at **Marquee** (▷ 132).

For top chart hits and great views over The Strip, try **OMNIA** (▷ 133).

For new innovations that will impress, join the sophisticated crowd at **XS** (▷ 135).

### World-Class Entertainment

Céline Dion is packing in the crowds again at the **Colosseum** in Caesars Palace (▷ 130). Make a reservation for a close encounter with a megastar; check out **Planet Hollywood** (▷ 127) to see who's making headlines.

See one of **Cirque du Soleil's** breathtaking spectacles, such as *Michael Jackson ONE* (▷ 132).

### Some Casino Action

Join the high rollers at **The Venetian** (▷ 58–59), watched over by Tiepolos and Titians.

Cocktail waitresses in short-skirted togas will serve you drinks at **Caesars Palace** (▷ 16–17) while you place your bets.

Tuxedo-backed chairs set the tone at **New York New York** (▷ 44–45), against the backdrop of the Big Apple.

*a stretch limousine is one of the classic ways to get around town; the Stratosphere Tower*

# Timeline

**1829** The spring at Las Vegas is discovered by a Mexican scout, Rafael Rivera, riding with a 60-strong trading party that had strayed from the Spanish Trail en route to Los Angeles.

**1855** Mormon settlers build a fort at Las Vegas. They stay for three years, until Native American raids drive them out.

### EARLY BEGINNINGS

In prehistoric times the land on which the city stands was a marshy area that supported vigorous plant life, but the water eventually receded and the arid landscape we see today was created. However, underground water occasionally surfaced to nourish an oasis on the site where Vegas now stands, known at that time only to the area's Native Americans. Archaeological finds just 10 miles (16km) northwest of Vegas have identified one of the oldest sites of human habitation in the United States. Items have been found at Tule Springs that date from around 11,000 to 14,000 years ago.

**1905** On May 15, the railroad arrives, and trackside lots in what is now the Fremont Street area sell like hot cakes.

**1910** Gambling is made illegal in the state of Nevada, sending the games underground.

**1931** The Nevada legislature passes a bill to allow gambling, and the Red Rooster becomes the first casino to open in Las Vegas. Nevada remains the only state to allow casino gambling until 1976, when casinos are introduced to Atlantic City, New Jersey.

**1940s** A building boom expands Las Vegas and more casinos come to town, along with organized crime. Vegas is ruled by the Mafia behind the scenes for decades.

**1946** The Flamingo, one of the foremost early casinos, opens its doors. It's financed by Benjamin "Bugsy" Siegel of the Meyer Lansky gang.

*"Bugsy" Siegel's Flamingo Hotel, c.1947*

*Demolition of the Stardust Resort and Casino on The Strip in 2007*

**1959** The Tropicana Hotel buys the American rights to the Parisian Folies Bergère show—it runs until 2009, with some 40,000 spectators a month.

**1960s** The Rat Pack (Frank Sinatra, Dean Martin, Sammy Davis Jr. *et al.*) arrive, setting the pattern for superstar entertainment.

**1967** The Nevada legislature approves a bill that allows publicly traded corporations to obtain gambling licenses. Legitimate money begins to loosen the Mafia's hold.

**1976** Casino gambling is legalized in Atlantic City; Las Vegas has competition.

**1990s** Las Vegas begins to promote family attractions. Ever bigger, more fantastic architecture starts to dominate The Strip.

**1999** Wayne Newton, "Mr Las Vegas," signs a lucrative contract with the Stardust Hotel.

**2004** A new state-of-the-art monorail opens.

**2005** On May 15, Las Vegas celebrates its 100th birthday.

**2012** Opening of the $485 million Smith Center for the Performing Arts, which hosts major Broadway shows, as well as orchestral, operatic, jazz and dance performances.

**2013** Caesars opens The LINQ, a giant new entertainment complex on The Strip, featuring the world's tallest observation wheel (550ft/168m).

**2016** Opened in 1955, the Riviera Hotel and Casino is the latest hotel to be imploded on The Strip.

### EVERYONE'S A WINNER

The fortunes of Las Vegas owe a lot to entrepreneur and property developer Steve Wynn (b.1942). Raised in New York, he took over the family bingo business in the 1960s and moved to Las Vegas in 1967. His first major venture here was to revamp the Golden Nugget. His next project was The Mirage casino resort, which opened in 1989, followed by Treasure Island in 1993. Next came Bellagio, spawning a new breed of luxury resorts. When his company Mirage Resorts was sold to MGM Grand Inc. in 2000, he turned his energies to his most expensive development, the Wynn Las Vegas, followed by the Encore next door. Wynn became a billionaire by 2004 and is an ardent art collector.

*Steve Wynn, CEO of Wynn Resorts*

# Top 25

This section contains the must-see Top 25 sights and experiences in Las Vegas. They are listed alphabetically, and numbered so you can locate them on the inside front cover map.

# ★1 Bellagio

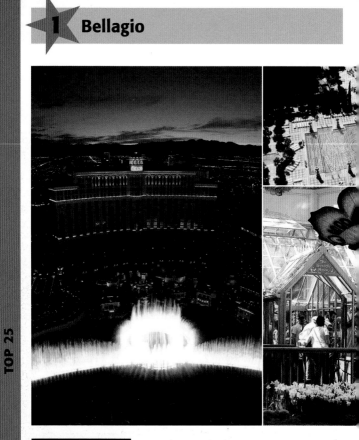

The Italianate image for this $1.6 billion
hotel, deemed to be one of the most
opulent resorts in the world, was inspired
by a village on the shores of Lake Como.

**A touch of class** An 8.5-acre (3.5ha) artificial
lake at the front of the hotel sets the stage for
the elegance, art and grandeur that awaits
you inside. The dazzling front lobby has an
18ft (5.5m) ceiling with a central chandelier
of glass flowers called Fiori di Como, designed
by sculptor Dale Chihuly. All this splendor is
enhanced by the wonderful botanical garden,
set under a glass atrium.

**Fountains of Bellagio** During the computer-
controlled, choreographed fountain show,
millions of gallons of water are sprayed to

*Clockwise from far left: View of the Bellagio from the Eiffel Tower at Paris Las Vegas; the Bellagio's pools; Dale Chihuly's spectacular lobby ceiling and chandelier of glass flowers; the plants in the indoor conservatory change seasonally*

heights of 240ft (73m) above the hotel's massive lake. The system uses individually programmed water jets and atomizing nozzles that create an atmospheric fog on the lake; some jets change the direction of the water in time to music ranging from Pavarotti to Sinatra, creating a dancing effect. At night the show is enhanced by state-of-the-art illumination and superb audio.

**Over the top** The casino oozes sophistication and style throughout, as even its slot machines are encased in marble and wood. Bellagio is also proud of its Gallery of Fine Art (▷ 69), and its theater was styled after the Paris Opera for Cirque du Soleil's "O" (▷ 132). The glass-enclosed Via Bellagio shopping arcade (▷ 123) has exclusive boutiques.

### THE BASICS

bellagio.com
✚ C9–D9
✉ 3600 Las Vegas Boulevard South
☎ 702/693-7111
⏱ Fountains: Mon–Fri 3pm–midnight, Sat–Sun 12–12; every half-hour to 7 or 8pm then every 15 min (may be canceled in high winds); Conservatory: daily 24hr
🍴 Several cafés and restaurants $$–$$$
🚌 Bally's/Paris
🚍 Deuce, SDX
♿ Very good
💲 Fountains & conservatory: free; art gallery moderate
❓ No under-18s allowed unless accompanied by an adult

# 2 Caesars Palace and The Forum Shops

### HIGHLIGHTS

● The Forum Shops mall
● Festival of Fountains
● A performance at the Colosseum

So you're in Las Vegas, and the thing you most want to do is spend a day shopping for Euro-designer chic surrounded by the historic buildings of Ancient Rome? No problem. It's all here at Caesars Palace.

**Classical architecture** Imagine that you have been transported to the Italian capital, amid imitative architecture that spans the period from 300BC to AD1700. The grounds are filled with reproductions of Roman statues, marble columns and colonnades, and toga-clad cocktail waitresses and costumed centurions tend to your every need in the exciting casino.

**The Forum Shops** Visit the phenomenal retail concourse, The Forum Shops. Browse stores such as Burberry and Tiffany & Co., or eat at

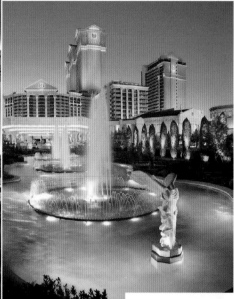

*Clockwise from far left: The Fountain of the Gods; a replica of Michelangelo's* David; *nighttime view of the hotel; The Forum Shops mall*

one of the many restaurants. An artificial sky overhead lightens and darkens, giving the illusion that 24 hours have passed in just one hour. Every hour in the Roman Great Hall, cinematic special effects and giant-sized animatronic statues combine to portray the struggle to rule Atlantis. All this happens against a backdrop of a 50,000-gallon saltwater aquarium in which hundreds of different species of tropical fish swim.

**Star-studded performances** The massive 4,300-seat Colosseum (▷ 130) has hosted many big-name artists, including Céline Dion and Elton John. Other attractions reserved for hotel guests include the Garden of the Gods pool oasis, where you can relax, enjoy a drink and play swim-up blackjack.

## THE BASICS

caesarspalace.com

➕ C8–D8

✉ 3570 Las Vegas Boulevard South

☎ 702/731-7110.
The Forum Shops: 702/893-4800

🕐 Atlantis show: daily every hour 10am–10pm or 11pm

🍴 Several cafés and restaurants $–$$$

🚌 Flamingo/Caesars Palace

🚏 Deuce

♿ Very good

✋ Atlantis show: free

# ★3 CityCenter

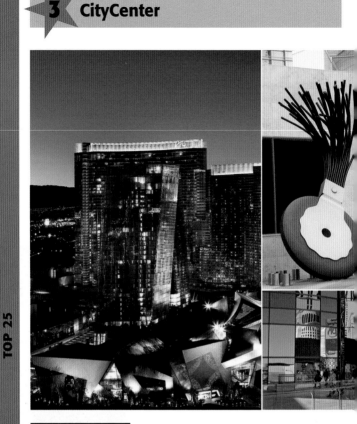

This ultra-modern complex of gleaming angular towers is a self-contained city in the heart of The Strip. It's architecturally stunning, setting new standards for style and sophistication.

**Layout** CityCenter comprises three hotels: the Aria, Vdara and the Mandarin Oriental. The site includes Crystals, the first retail center to be designed by architect Daniel Libeskind, as well as its own power plant, fire station and tram line. The complex was built with special attention to energy conservation. It uses its excess electricity to provide its hot water, and its stretch limos run on compressed natural gas—a world first. Aria has a fabulous, state-of-the-art spa featuring Japanese-style heated stone beds.

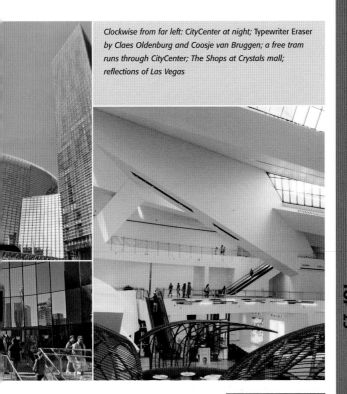

*Clockwise from far left: CityCenter at night; Typewriter Eraser by Claes Oldenburg and Coosje van Bruggen; a free tram runs through CityCenter; The Shops at Crystals mall; reflections of Las Vegas*

**Arty refuge** CityCenter's towers are grouped around spacious plazas and atriums, which are decorated with artworks by internationally acclaimed artists, such as Henry Moore, Claes Oldenburg, Maya Lin, Richard Long, Nancy Rubins and Frank Stella. Giant aerial sculptures hang from cavernous hallways, and miniature whirlpools gyrate inside glass tubes embedded in the sidewalk. Among the most spectacular pieces are Nancy Rubins' *Big Edge*—a spiky sculpture of boats and canoes outside Vdara; Maya Lin's *Silver River*, suspended over Aria's registration desk; and a large marble sculpture by Henry Moore in the walkway, between the Aria and Crystals. The wide open public spaces offer a more relaxed experience, with modern art on display and fountains that both stimulate and soothe the senses.

### THE BASICS

aria.com

➕ C9–D10

✉ 3730 Las Vegas Boulevard South

☎ 702/590-7111 (Aria), 866/359-7111 (Aria toll-free), 702/590-2111 (Vdara), 866/745-7111 (Vdara toll-free), 702/590-8888 (Mandarin Oriental)

🍴 Numerous restaurants and cafés $–$$$

🚏 Bally's/Paris

🚌 Deuce

♿ Very good

🎨 Art exhibits: free

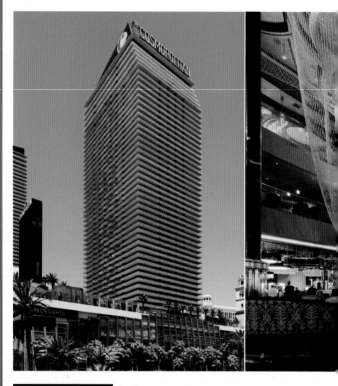

## HIGHLIGHTS

● The Chandelier
● Marquee nightclub

## TIPS

● Marquee nightclub also operates as a dayclub, the latest trend in 24/7 Vegas.
● On some summer evenings, you can watch a movie while you swim with Dive-In Movies at the Boulevard Pool, usually at 7.30pm.

The Cosmopolitan is a gleaming, ultra-modern luxury hotel and casino, whose sophisticated amenities and bevy of edgy restaurants and nightspots reflect its fashionable, stylish image.

**The building** Overlooking The Strip between the Bellagio and CityCenter, Cosmopolitan is formed of two square-sided, elegant glass-encased towers. Inside are nearly 3,000 sumptuous boutique-style apartments, bungalows and suites. The special attractions are the nightlife and the spectacular Chandelier.

**The Chandelier** This shimmering cylindrical curtain contains two million glass beads, whose effect is technically enhanced with digitally programmed lighting effects. Within this fantasy

*Far left: The Cosmopolitan, a striking addition to the Las Vegas scene; below: the spectacular three-level Chandelier is unlike any bar you have ever been in*

world are a bar, lounge and cocktail bar. You can choose between DJ entertainment on the bottom level, colorful cocktails in the middle, or intimately cosy sofas on the top-floor lounge.

**Nightclubs, pools and more** Clustered around the Chandelier are Cosmopolitan's many amenities, both for night-owls and daytime visitors. Its hottest nightspot is the Marquee Nightclub, with huge four-story LED displays around its vast dance floor. For eating options, you can choose from simple snack outlets to gourmet celebrity-chef restaurants. Among the top venues are José Andrés' Jaleo restaurant (▷ 144), and Momofuku (▷ 146). There are three pools, or if you're in the mood to splurge, there are some very swanky shops here, and a casino.

## THE BASICS

cosmopolitanlasvegas.com

✛ D9

✉ 3708 Las Vegas Boulevard South

☎ 702/698-7000

🕒 Boulevard Pool: seasonally, hours vary; Marquee nightclub: Mon, Fri & Sat 10.30pm–5am; Marquee Dayclub: Apr–Oct daily 11.30am–sunset

🍴 Cafés and restaurants

🚇 Bally's/Paris

🚌 Deuce

♿ Very good

🎨 Art exhibits: free

**21**

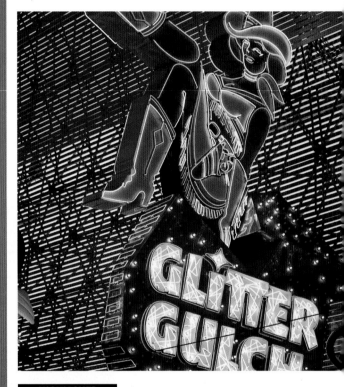

### HIGHLIGHTS

● Fremont Street
Experience (▷ 24)
● Main Street Station
(▷ 156)
● Golden Nugget (▷ 69)
● The Neon Museum
(▷ 42)

### TIP

● Some of the carts on the
Fremont Street Experience
have unusual gift and
souvenir items for sale.

With its old-world appeal, Downtown is
where the spirit of Las Vegas' humble
beginnings still lives on through vintage
casino hotels like the Plaza, the Golden
Nugget and the Golden Gate, the city's
oldest hotel.

**Origins** Centered on Fremont Street between
Main Street and Las Vegas Boulevard, the
streets of Downtown are more low-key and
less glamorous than those on The Strip. In the
1920s, Fremont Street was the first street in
Las Vegas to be paved and have traffic lights,
and by the 1930s it had the first licensed
gaming hall. Downtown already had 36 years
of history as the commercial heart of Vegas by
the time the first casino resort, El Rancho, was
built on The Strip in 1941.

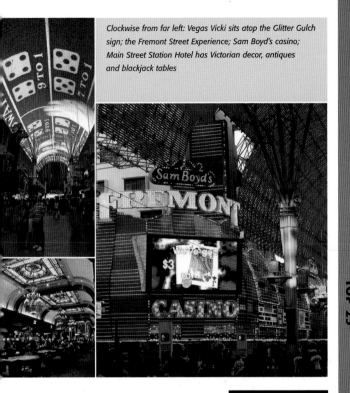

*Clockwise from far left: Vegas Vicki sits atop the Glitter Gulch sign; the Fremont Street Experience; Sam Boyd's casino; Main Street Station Hotel has Victorian decor, antiques and blackjack tables*

**Revitalization** Downtown had lost much of its business to The Strip by the 1990s, but since then the $70 million Fremont Street Experience (▷ 24–25) has succeeded in bringing in the punters once again and putting Glitter Gulch— as it is known—firmly back on the map.

**More attractions** With its striking Victorian decor and genuine antiques, Main Street Station (▷ 156) has one of Downtown's best casinos in terms of comfort and atmosphere. Inside the Golden Nugget casino (▷ 69), snap a photo of the Hand of Faith, an enormous (875 troy oz) gold nugget found in Australia, and The Tank, a 200,000-gallon aquarium filled with sharks and tropical fish. The shark tank has a thrilling glass-enclosed waterslide that hotel guests can ride.

### THE BASICS

➕ G2–G3
✉ Centered around Fremont and Main Street between Main Street and Las Vegas Boulevard
🍴 Many cafés, restaurants and snack bars $–$$$
🚌 108, Deuce
♿ Good

**DID YOU KNOW?**

● Fremont Street was the hub of Las Vegas for nearly four decades.

● Each column supporting the overhead structure carries 400,000lb (181,440kg) of weight.

● The components for the light show produce 65,536 color combinations.

● The show's sound system generates 550,000 watts.

Head north to Downtown Las Vegas (▷ 22–23) after dark to see the only show of its kind in the world—a fantastic light-and-sound show on a massive frame that overarches a five-block area.

**High-tech marvel** The specifications for the initial display comprised 2 million light bulbs, with strobe lighting added to enhance the disco nights. In 2004, a $17 million upgrade provided a 12.5 million LED light display and a better quality system (to 550,000 watts) for state-of-the-art sound.

**Under cover of lightness** The Experience is a high-tech phenomenon with the latest computers intertwining the light, visual and audio systems. This glittering spectacular is

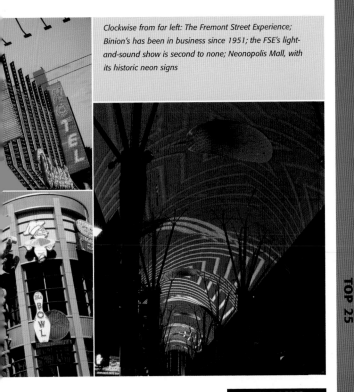

Clockwise from far left: The Fremont Street Experience; Binion's has been in business since 1951; the FSE's light-and-sound show is second to none; Neonopolis Mall, with its historic neon signs

based on a huge, solid frame that curves 90ft (27m) above traffic-free Fremont Street, between Main and 4th streets. A number of the Downtown casinos are within this area (▷ 22–23), adding to the overall effect with their illuminated facades. There are 16 massive columns and 43,000 struts supporting the frame, but once the show starts you will be totally focused on this zany experience that has been wowing the crowds here since 1995.

**By day** You might think it's rather dull here during the day, but the display frame shelters a lively shopping mall, the sound system pipes in music to shop by, and there are often free concerts and street performers. SlotZilla, a new zip line, 114ft (35m) above the street, offers high-adrenaline thrills (▷ 73).

## THE BASICS

vegasexperience.com
➕ G3
✉ Fremont Street
☎ 702/678-5600
🕐 Shows nightly on the hour every hour from dusk to midnight (1am in summer)
🍴 Restaurants and snack bars $–$$$
🚌 Deuce, SDX, WAX
♿ Very good
🎟 Free

### HIGHLIGHTS

● Guided tour into the
Hoover Dam
● Cruising Lake Mead on
an organized sightseeing
tour

### TIPS

● There is a large choice
of tours available from Las
Vegas (▷ 167).
● The best sightseeing
cruise on Lake Mead is the
one aboard the *Desert
Princess*.
● Tours of the dam leave
from the exhibit center at
the top of the dam.

It's hard to visit Vegas without feeling some
wonderment about the power it must
take to light up the town. You'll find some
answers at Hoover Dam, and while you're
out of the city, enjoy a cruise on the lovely
lake it created.

**A marvel of engineering** Without the Hoover
Dam, Las Vegas, as we know it, would not
exist. Constructed in the mid-1930s to control
flooding on the Colorado River, it also provides
drinking water for 18 million people and electricity for half a million homes. It was completed
two years ahead of schedule. At the peak of
construction more than 5,000 people were
employed and 96 workers died on the project.
Fascinating tours take visitors deep inside the
structure to learn about its inner workings.

Clockwise from far left: On the shores of Lake Mead;
Hoover Dam, once the largest dam in the world;
the dam's structural volume surpasses that of the
largest pyramid in Egypt; the Desert Princess *tour boat*

**Lovely Lake Mead** The damming of the
Colorado River beginning in 1935 created the
largest artificial lake in the US at the time, with
a vast 550-mile (885km) shoreline. There's a
scenic drive along the western side, and the
Alan Bible Visitor Center, just west of the dam,
has information about waterborne activities.
There are five marinas, and you can rent a boat
or jet ski, go fishing, water-skiing or swimming.
On dry land, there are lakeshore walks and
facilities for camping and picnicking. Boulder
City, near the lakeshore, was built to house
the dam's construction workers and was "dry"
(no alcohol or gambling). It is now the only
community in Nevada that still restricts gambling. A new highway, bypassing the dam, was
built in 2010, to help to ease traffic to and from
the Grand Canyon.

## THE BASICS

usbr.gov/lc/hoover
dam; nps.gov

➕ See map ▷ 109

✉ 30 miles (48km)
southeast of Las Vegas

☎ Hoover Dam tours:
702/494-2517; Alan Bible
Visitor Center: 702/293-
8990; Lake Mead Cruises:
866/292-9191

🕐 Hoover Dam Visitor
Center: daily 9–6 (5 in
winter); Alan Bible Visitor
Center: daily 9–4.30

✋ Hoover Dam Visitor
Center Tours: expensive;
Lake Mead Recreation
Area: inexpensive; Lake
Mead cruise: expensive

● Views from the top of High Roller
● Live music at Brooklyn Bowl

TIPS

● Daytime rides (before 5pm) on High Roller are less expensive
● Advance online tickets for High Roller are often discounted

Rising an impressive 550ft (168m) above The Strip, Vegas' sleek High Roller currently holds the envied title of the world's largest observation wheel and is taller than both the London Eye and the Singapore Flyer.

**Superlative views** Opened in 2014, the High Roller has changed the skyline of The Strip. It takes 30 minutes for the wheel to complete a full revolution, giving passengers plenty of time to soak up the views of Las Vegas Boulevard and the desert mountains bordering the Las Vegas Valley. Each of the wheel's 28 glass-enclosed cabins can hold up to 40 people. Views of The Strip's neon lights are mesmerizing at night, when the wheel is itself lit up with 2,000 LED lights.

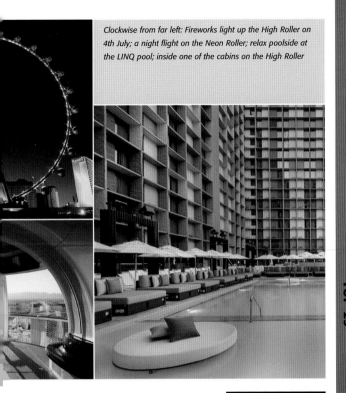

*Clockwise from far left: Fireworks light up the High Roller on 4th July; a night flight on the Neon Roller; relax poolside at the LINQ pool; inside one of the cabins on the High Roller*

**Do it differently** This is Vegas, where everything keeps getting bigger, flashier and more entertaining. VIP experiences available on the High Roller wheel (which must be booked in advance) include "Yoga in the Sky," chocolate and wine tasting extravaganzas, and even wedding ceremonies that let couples exchange vows inside a private cabin.

**Linking up** High Roller stands at the end of The LINQ Promenade (▷ 120), an open-air pedestrian passageway lined with boutique shops, restaurants and bars that's named for The LINQ Hotel & Casino (▷ 156) next door. At Brooklyn Bowl, a New York City import, visitors come not just for bowling, but for cocktails, all-American comfort food and indie concerts. Step out onto the upstairs balcony for photo ops.

## THE BASICS

caesars.com/linq

✚ D8–D9

✉ 3535 Las Vegas Boulevard South

☎ 702/322-0593

🕐 The Linq: daily 24 hours; High Roller: daily 11.30am–2am

🍴 Several cafés and restaurants $–$$$

🚇 Harrah's/The LINQ

🚌 Deuce

♿ Very good

💰 Expensive

## HIGHLIGHTS

- *Bodies...The Exhibition*
- *Titanic* exhibition
- Replica Sphinx
- Laser light

## TIP

● Save your aching feet and take the free tram to Luxor, which runs between Excalibur and Mandalay Bay every 3–7 minutes (daily, 9am–10.30pm).

Stare slack-jawed at the stunning Ancient Egyptian exterior of this vast resort. Inside its cavernous interior are two of the most imaginative and cutting-edge exhibitions you'll find in Vegas.

**Egyptian roots** Although more modern attractions are on offer inside, the black-glass pyramid, with its 10-floor replica Sphinx at the entrance to the main hotel building, still dominates. A narrow spotlight shoots out from the top of the pyramid; claimed to be the strongest beam of light in the world, on a clear night it is visible from planes passing overhead.

***Titanic* docks at Luxor** *Titanic: The Artifact Exhibition* takes you on an emotional journey back in time to experience the ill-fated ship's

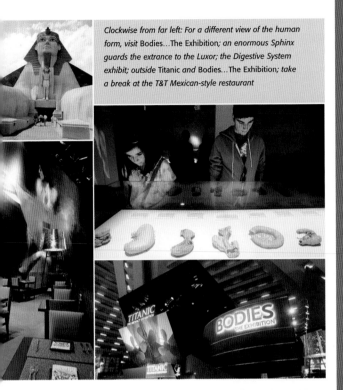

Clockwise from far left: For a different view of the human form, visit Bodies...The Exhibition; an enormous Sphinx guards the entrance to the Luxor; the Digestive System exhibit; outside Titanic and Bodies...The Exhibition; take a break at the T&T Mexican-style restaurant

maiden voyage. On display are hundreds of authentic objects recovered from *Titanic's* final resting place. A reconstructed ship's bow utilizes a moving lifeboat to gain access on board. Walk through accurate room re-creations, share in the real-life stories of the passengers and crew, and experience the feel of an iceberg, which all sets the stage for one of history's greatest tragedies.

**Come see what's inside** *Bodies...The Exhibition* is a superb opportunity to see the inner workings of our bodies through actual preserved human bodies, plus more than 260 organs and partial body specimens. This daring attraction is a groundbreaking venture for Las Vegas—a fairly serious experience that will leave you with many lasting thoughts.

## THE BASICS

luxor.com

C11–D11

3900 Las Vegas Boulevard South

702/262-4000

*Titanic* and *Bodies* exhibitions: daily 10–10

Several cafés and restaurants

MGM Grand

Deuce

Very good

*Titanic* and *Bodies* exhibitions: expensive

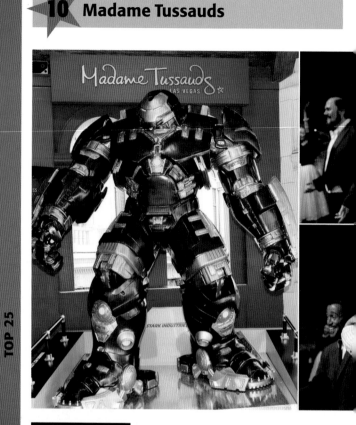

### HIGHLIGHTS

● "Music Icons"
● "The Hangover Experience"
● "Viva Vegas"
● "Marvel Superheroes"

It is fitting that Madame Tussauds' flashiest foray into the United States should be in Las Vegas, a magnet for both the biggest showbiz personalities and the most ardent celebrity-spotters.

**Making an impression** Madame Tussauds is the world leader when it comes to making realistic likenesses in wax of the rich, the famous, and the infamous. The secret to the waxworks' life-like appearance is that they are made from an impression from the real person, rather than simply using an artist's sculpture, so every detail is absolutely spot on. This can be a rather claustrophobic experience; Napoleon was famously freaked out by it. Today, however, most celebrities regard it as one of the signs that they have really made it in show business.

*The star-studded cast at Madame Tussauds includes (clockwise from far left): Ironman, Louis Armstrong, Muhammad Ali, Marilyn Monroe and Frank Sinatra*

**Las Vegas legends** Not surprisingly, pride of place here goes to the superstars who have made their mark in Las Vegas—Wayne Newton, Elvis Presley, Céline Dion and the Rat Pack, to name just a few but the collection regularly evolves as new stars are born. Among more than 100 other masterfully produced figures is a glittering, international cast of movie and TV stars, icons from the music world and sport's biggest achievers.

**Interactive experience** Some of the exhibits allow you to interact with the famous models by taking part in a scenario, such as auditioning in front of Simon Cowell for *American Idol*, playing hoops with NBA superstar Shaquille O'Neal or stepping onto a TV studio set with Jerry Springer.

## THE BASICS

madametussauds.com/las-vegas

➕ D8

✉ The Venetian, 3377 Las Vegas Boulevard South

☎ 702/862-7800

🕐 Sun–Thu 10–9, Fri–Sat 10–10 (closes early in winter and for special events)

🍴 Several cafés and restaurants at The Venetian $–$$$

🚌 Harrah's/The LINQ

🚍 Deuce

♿ Excellent

💲 Expensive

TOP 25

### HIGHLIGHTS

● MGM Lion outside the main entrance
● CSI: The Experience
● Wet Republic
● *KÀ*, Cirque du Soleil's Egyptian-inspired extravaganza
● Joël Robuchon, 3-Michelin star restaurant

### TIP

● Hop on the monorail (▷ 167). to get to and from other major resorts.

One of the vaunted landmarks of The Strip, the MGM Grand has added an extra sparkle of Hollywood glitz since it opened in 1993.

**The lion** Probably the first thing you'll see when you arrive at the front entrance is the giant bronze lion statue, the instantly recognizable symbol of MGM movies since 1924. It stands 45ft (14m) tall and weighs 100,000 pounds (45,350kg).

**The Grand** MGM Grand is an impressive hotel casino buzzing with high-energy attractions and activities. Highlights include CSI: The Experience (▷ 67), an interactive crime-solving challenge based on the successful TV series; *KÀ* (▷ 132), one of Cirque du Soleil's most thrilling shows; and Wet Republic (▷ 74), a

Clockwise from far left: The entrance to The MGM Grand sports bar; the MGM Grand, with its iconic lion statue, has entertained visitors to Las Vegas for over 20 years; inside the lobby at the Joël Robuchon restaurant at The MGM Grand

pool club for the city's party people. If you prefer to splash about at a more relaxed pace, you can drift along Backlot River, or pamper yourself in the Grand Spa.

**Dine, dance and make merry** The many dining options are headed by the Joël Robuchon restaurant (▷ 144). Hakkasan (▷ 131) offers Michelin-star awarded Cantonese cuisine with innovative nightclub entertainment. MGM Grand Garden Arena is a major concert hall and entertainment venue, seating 16,800. It has hosted global stars, including the Rolling Stones, Bruce Springsteen, Madonna and, more recently, Lady Gaga, Coldplay and Jennifer Lopez. Sports contests also feature, including world championship boxing and basketball.

**THE BASICS**

mgmgrand.com
🔁 D10
✉ 3799 Las Vegas Boulevard South
☎ 702/891-1111
⊙ CSI: The Experience: daily 9–9
🍴 Several cafés and restaurants $–$$$
🚉 MGM Grand
🚌 Deuce
♿ Very good
🎟 CSI Experience: expensive

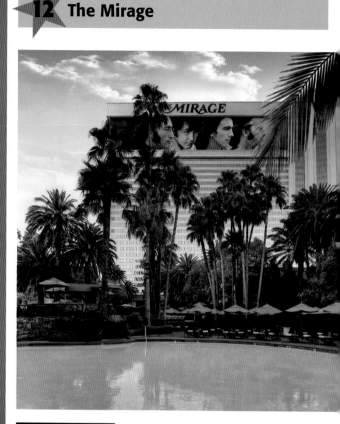

## HIGHLIGHTS

● Volcanic eruption
● Secret Garden and white tigers
● Dolphin Habitat

## TIPS

● Note that the volcano eruption will be canceled during bad weather or high winds.
● Take the free tram between Treasure Island (TI) and The Mirage (every 15 minutes, 7am–2am).

There is nothing quite as fascinating as an exotic spectacle, and watching The Mirage's simulated volcano erupt or coming face-to-face with magnificent wildlife will stop almost anyone in their tracks.

**Tropical delights** This Polynesian-style resort is fronted by cascading waterfalls, tropical foliage and an imitation volcano. As you enter the lobby, you can't miss the huge coral-reef aquarium stocked with tropical fish. Venture farther in and you will discover a lush rainforest under a large atrium.

**Eruptions to order** You can wait years for a real volcano to create its spectacle, but here, in front of The Mirage, you can set your watch by it. The newly renovated spectacular 4.5-minute

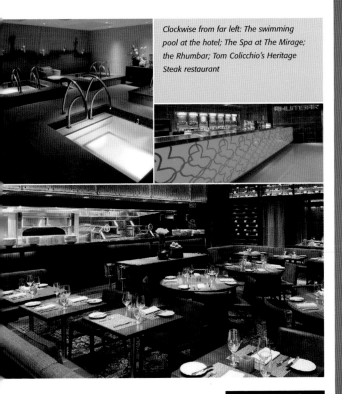

Clockwise from far left: The swimming pool at the hotel; The Spa at The Mirage; the Rhumbar; Tom Colicchio's Heritage Steak restaurant

show starts with a rumbling sound, then a fog swirls around and a column of smoke and fire shoots more than 12ft (3.5m) into the sky. The show includes the latest special effects, with real flames on the water of the lagoon and state-of-the-art lighting techniques and sound systems. Make sure you arrive early to get a front-row position.

**Other attractions** The Mirage is also home to Siegfried & Roy's Secret Garden and Dolphin Habitat (▷ 73). For more wildlife viewing, seek out the 20,000-gallon saltwater aquarium, filled with 85 species of colorful tropical fish, by the hotel registration desk. The Cirque du Soleil's *The Beatles: LOVE* (▷ 129), is presented at The Mirage and celebrates the musical legacy of the Fab Four.

## THE BASICS

mirage.com

✚ C8–D8

✉ 3400 Las Vegas Boulevard South

☎ 702/791-7111

🕐 Volcanic eruption: daily from 7pm (last showtime varies)

🍽 Several cafés and restaurants $–$$$

🚌 Harrah's/The LINQ

🚍 Deuce

♿ Excellent

🎫 Volcanic eruption: free

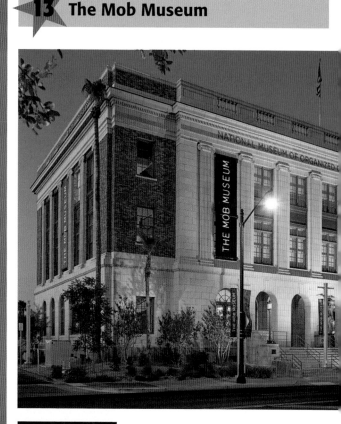

## HIGHLIGHTS

● The Barber's Chair—where "Murder Inc." mobster Albert Anastasia was shot dead in New York in 1957
● The wall from the 1929 St. Valentine's Day Massacre
● Mob-themed souvenirs from the gift shop

This historical museum aims to demystify the gangsters who fought for control of Las Vegas in its early days, and the lawmen who pursued them. It occupies three floors of a former federal courthouse and post office in Downtown.

**Historic site** Here, in 1950, the US Senate Special Committee held one of a series of nationwide hearings investigating the activities of organized crime. They found that the Capone Syndicate and New York Syndicate had turned organized crime into big business. The conclusions sent shock waves around the US, leading to the downfall of these infamous syndicates. The Mob Museum focuses on these historic events and re-creates real scenes involving the major players on both sides of the law.

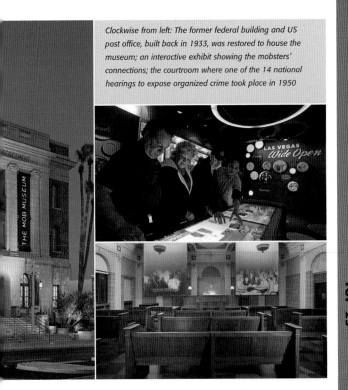

*Clockwise from left: The former federal building and US post office, built back in 1933, was restored to house the museum; an interactive exhibit showing the mobsters' connections; the courtroom where one of the 14 national hearings to expose organized crime took place in 1950*

**Skims and mayhem** There are a number of areas to the museum, also known as the Las Vegas Museum of Organized Crime and Law Enforcement, including: We Only Kill Each Other, Follow the Money, and Bringing Down the Mob. Displays include weapons used by mob hit-men in their grisly deeds, set against a backdrop of the museum's iconic artifact—the wall from Chicago's St. Valentine's Day Massacre. Other exhibits show how the casinos' profits were skimmed off and sent to crime syndicates' dens. Bringing Down the Mob focuses on wiretapping—one of the most important tools used to prosecute cases. Interactive exhibits allow you to listen in on and interpret coded conversations, examine photos and surveillance films and learn about witness protection programs.

TOP 25

### THE BASICS

themobmuseum.org
�"🔽 G2
✉ 300 Stewart Avenue, Downtown
☎ 702/229-2734
🕐 Daily 9–9
🚌 Deuce
♿ Very good
💲 Expensive

# 14 National Atomic Testing Center

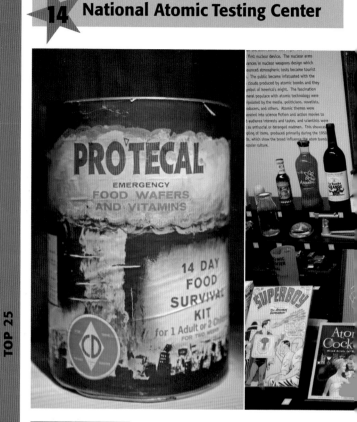

● Ground Zero Theater
● A piece of the Berlin Wall
● Atomic Age cultural exhibits

This was the first museum of its kind in the US. It provides fascinating insight into scientific work done at the Nevada Test Site starting in the wake of WWII and its subsequent global impact.

**In depth** Less than 2 miles (3km) east of The Strip, this museum is certainly something different and a long way from the usual superficial hype of Las Vegas casinos. Interactive exhibits help you learn about the history of nuclear power, and you can experience a simulated atomic explosion in the Ground Zero Theater. Other displays show you more about "backpack nukes," nuclear missiles, underground testing and radiation measurement, as well as pop culture and everyday life during the Cold War era.

Exhibits at the National Atomic Testing Museum documenting the history of nuclear testing at the Nevada Test Site (NTS)

**Telling a story** At the museum entrance, the ticket booth is a replica of a guard station at the historic Nevada Test Site. Located 100 miles (160km) northwest of Las Vegas out in the desert, this site was a premier proving ground for nuclear devices, and atmospheric tests were carried out there between 1951–62. During that time, mushroom clouds were visible on the horizon from casinos on The Strip, where viewing parties complete with live bands and atomic-themed cocktails often were held.

**Special attractions** The museum's temporary exhibits take a different look at Nevada's history, sometimes from an artistic point of view or at other times with a light-hearted approach, for example, examining the alien lore surrounding mysterious Area 51.

### THE BASICS

nationalatomictesting
museum.org
🚹 F9
✉ 755 East Flamingo
Road
☎ 702/794-5151
🕐 Mon–Sat 10–5,
Sun 12–5
🚌 202
♿ Very good
💲 Expensive

# ⭐15 The Neon Museum

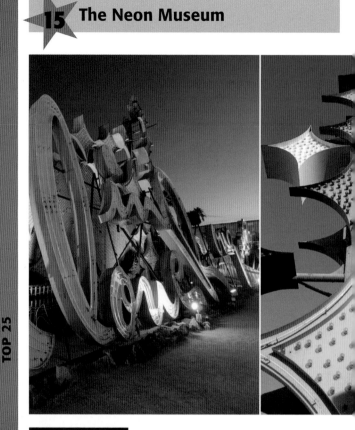

- Neon Boneyard tours
- La Concha Motel lobby

**TIPS**

- Advance booking recommended for tours (especially night tours)
- Inclement weather may cancel tours

Delve into Las Vegas' scandalous and storied history on a guided tour of the intriguing Neon Boneyard, a collection of more than 200 vintage signs salvaged from around the city.

**Touring the collection** Some of the most recognizable signs from decades past have found a new home at this outdoor museum, including Binion's lucky horseshoe, the flamboyant marquee from the now-departed Stardust casino and a sparkling, giant-sized high heel from the Silver Slipper casino. Daytime tours of the Boneyard are less expensive, but after-dark walks are more memorable, when a few of the restored signs are turned on and others are dramatically lit by floodlights. Tour tickets usually go on sale one month in advance.

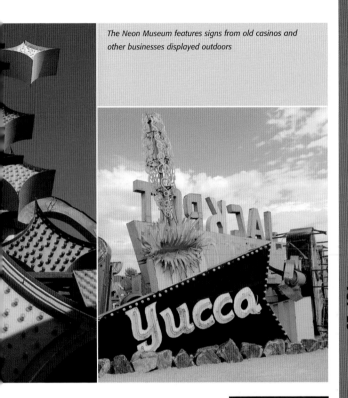

The Neon Museum features signs from old casinos and other businesses displayed outdoors

**Get the low-down** For more information and to inquire about last-minute tour availability, stop by the museum's Visitor Center, inside the refurbished La Concha Motel lobby. Designed by architect Paul Revere Williams, this shell-shaped building is an outstanding example of mid-20th-century Googie architecture.

**Around Downtown** If you don't have time to take a guided tour, you can still enjoy the Urban Gallery. Ten of the city's neon signs dating back to 1940 have been refurbished and displayed as installation art, on or just off Las Vegas Boulevard, between Sahara Avenue on the North Strip and Washington Avenue. More vintage neon signs are installed around the Neonopolis on the Fremont Street Experience pedestrian mall, viewable 24/7 for free.

### THE BASICS

neonmuseum.org
✚ H2
✉ 770 Las Vegas
Boulevard North
☎ 702/387-6366
🕐 Guided tours of Neon
Boneyard offered daily
(schedules vary)
🚌 113, 215
♿ Very good
💵 Moderate–expensive

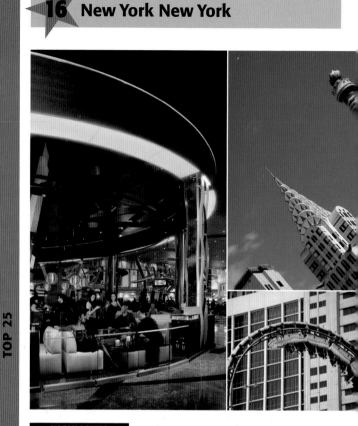

## HIGHLIGHTS

- Big Apple Coaster
- Statue of Liberty
- Brooklyn Bridge
- *Bliss Dance* sculpture in The Park

See the sights of the Big Apple in a fraction of the time you would need to explore the real thing. The Statue of Liberty, Brooklyn Bridge, the Chrysler Building—they are all here.

**New York in miniature** This fabulous resort hotel depicts the New York skyline through ingenious, scaled-down replicas—about one-third of the actual size—of famous Manhattan landmarks. The Statue of Liberty sits side by side with skyscrapers such as the Empire State Building and a 300ft-long (91m), 50ft-high (15m) version of the Brooklyn Bridge. The hotel's elegant art-deco lobby is set against representations of Times Square, Little Italy and Wall Street, and the casino is a nod to Central Park.

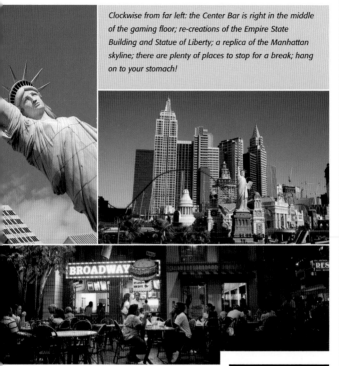

*Clockwise from far left: the Center Bar is right in the middle of the gaming floor; re-creations of the Empire State Building and Statue of Liberty; a replica of the Manhattan skyline; there are plenty of places to stop for a break; hang on to your stomach!*

**White-knuckle ride** The Big Apple Coaster twists, loops and dives at speeds of up to 67mph (108kph). The ride turns passengers upside down and inside out when the train drops 144ft (44m). This ride was the first to introduce the "heartline" twist and dive move, where riders experience weightlessness— the train rolls 180 degrees, suspending its passengers 86ft (26m) above the casino roof, before taking a sudden and stomach-churning dive.

**The Park** Next door is a vast outdoor entertainment complex with bars, restaurants, and the T-Mobile Arena for concerts and sporting events. Rising above the crowds is *Bliss Dance*, a 40ft-tall (12m) sculpture inspired by the Burning Man festival, held in Nevada's desert.

**THE BASICS**

newyorknewyork.com

🚇 D10

✉ 3790 Las Vegas Boulevard South

☎ 702/740-6969

🎟 Big Apple Coaster: daily 10.30am–midnight

🍴 Several cafés and restaurants $–$$$

🚉 MGM Grand

🚌 Deuce, SDX

♿ Very good

💲 Big Apple Coaster: moderate

❓ You must be at least 54in (1.37m) to ride the Big Apple Coaster

45

## HIGHLIGHTS

● Views from the Eiffel Tower Observation Deck
● Elegant shopping at Le Boulevard

Striving to capture the Parisian style of the most elegant of European cities, this hotel has succeeded in creating fine likenesses of the Eiffel Tower, Arc de Triomphe, Paris Opera House and the Louvre.

**Joie de vivre** This eye-catching resort may not be the real thing, but a characteristic French exuberance is reflected in little touches like café waiters dressed in striped shirts and berets, or maybe a "Bonjour!" from the hotel concierge.

**Eiffel Tower Experience** The symbol of this hotel is the 540ft (165m) Eiffel Tower (half the size of the original), which was recreated using Gustav Eiffel's blueprints. A glass elevator takes you to the observation deck on the 46th floor for spectacular views of Las Vegas

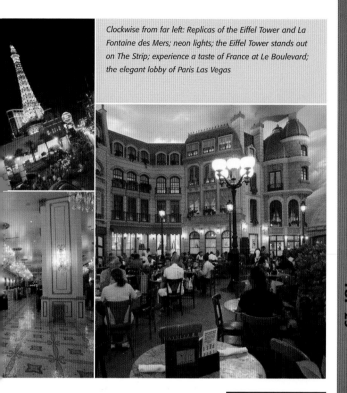

Clockwise from far left: Replicas of the Eiffel Tower and La Fontaine des Mers; neon lights; the Eiffel Tower stands out on The Strip; experience a taste of France at Le Boulevard; the elegant lobby of Paris Las Vegas

and the surrounding mountains—impressive at dusk when The Strip lights up and a prime lookout for the Bellagio fountain display opposite (▷ 14–15). Below on the 11th floor you can dine in the sophisticated, if pricey, Eiffel Tower Restaurant.

**Le Boulevard** Don't miss this French-style shopping boulevard. The retail space connects Paris Las Vegas to Bally's Las Vegas (▷ 154), the resort's sister property. Amid atmospheric winding alleyways and cobbled streets, the ornate facades conceal elegant French shops, boutiques and restaurants. Weathered brickwork and brass lamps give an authentic finish, and window boxes overflowing with bright blooms complete the Parisian picture. It's a unique shopping experience.

## THE BASICS

parislasvegas.com

➕ D9

✉ 3655 Las Vegas Boulevard South

☎ 702/946-7000

🕐 Eiffel Tower Experience: Mon–Fri 9.30am–12.30am, Sat–Sun 9.30am–1am (weather permitting)

🍴 Several cafés and restaurants $–$$$

🚊 Bally's/Paris

🚌 Deuce

♿ Very good

💲 Eiffel Tower Experience: moderate

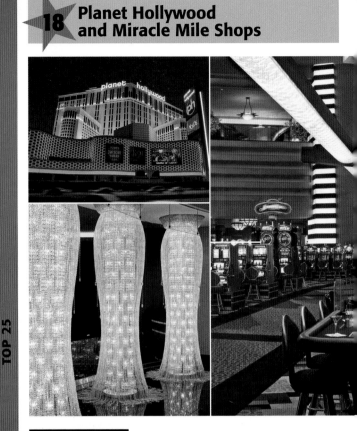

## HIGHLIGHTS

● The indoor rainstorm
● The Miracle Mile Shops

Planet Hollywood has made a successful transition from Middle Eastern-themed hotel to the bright, brash style of Hollywood with a modern feel.

**Just like Times Square** Massive LED signs with continually flashing images light up this part of The Strip, and when you step inside the Planet, as it's known, you will find an even more dramatic scene of highly polished black-granite floors and a color-shifting backdrop. The casino pulls in a young, svelte crowd, especially at the Pleasure Pit, where go-go girls dance above the gaming tables.

**Shopping with a difference** Make no mistake, Miracle Mile Shops is a shopping mall, with 170 international retailers, many eateries and a

*Clockwise from far left: Outside Planet Hollywood; roulette table in the casino; you may find yourself in the middle of a rainstorm as you shop at the Miracle Mile Shops; Planet Hollywood's opulent lobby*

plethora of entertainment venues, but it is not just an ordinary retail experience. It has a silver grid ceiling painted with fluffy clouds and a blue sky, which darkens during the day to complete the virtual reality effect. While you're there, check out the latest performances at the V Theater (▷ 135), which is owned by famed producer David Saxe and hosts a huge array of shows.

**Stormy weather** Miracle Mile Shops is also home to the bustling Merchant's Harbor, complete with the gentle sounds of lapping waves. At intervals you will hear the rumble of distant thunder as a storm begins to brew. Clouds gather and gentle rain falls on the harbor, although you won't need an umbrella from your viewpoint on the shore.

## THE BASICS

caesars.com/
planethollywood
miraclemileshopslv.com

➕ D9

✉ 3667 Las Vegas Boulevard South

☎ 702/785-5555

🕐 Miracle Mile Shops: Sun–Thu 10am–11pm, Fri–Sat 10am–midnight; rainstorm every hour on the hour Mon–Thu 10am–11pm, every half hour Fri–Sun 10am–11pm

🍴 Several cafés and restaurants $–$$$

🚇 Bally's/Paris

🚌 Deuce

♿ Very good

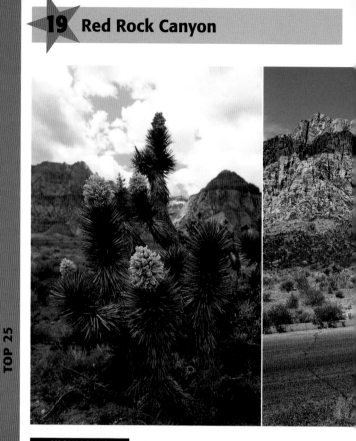

- Scenic Drive
- Hiking trails
- Children's Discovery Trail
- Wildlife—burros (wild donkeys) and desert big-horn sheep (hard to spot)

- Don't feed the wildlife; the burros may bite or kick.
- Take plenty of water if hiking—the heat can be fierce—and wear extra layers of clothes in winter.

This canyon was created 65 million years ago when the Keystone Thrust Fault pushed one rock plate up over another. The resulting formations, in gray limestone and red sandstone, are awesome.

**Focal point**  It's incredible to think that this striking canyon, set in the 196,000-acre (79,245ha) Red Rock Canyon National Conservation Area, is a mere 30-minute drive from the razzmatazz of Vegas. The focal point is the steep red rock escarpment, more than 13 miles (21km) long and almost 3,000ft (915m) high. More canyons have been gouged out within the formation by constant snowmelt and rains, creating the present dramatic land-scape. In contrast to the dry desert, springs and streams encourage lush vegetation.

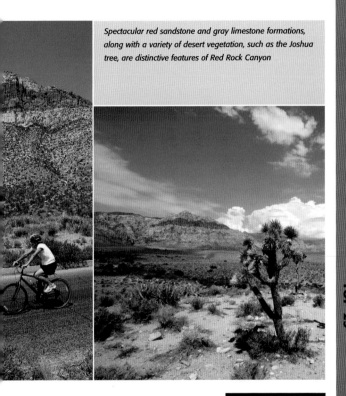

*Spectacular red sandstone and gray limestone formations, along with a variety of desert vegetation, such as the Joshua tree, are distinctive features of Red Rock Canyon*

**Planning ahead** The best place to start is at the Red Rock Canyon Visitor Center, which offers information and interpretation about all the recreational opportunities, including horseback riding, hiking and climbing. It also sells a recorded self-guide tour with a description of the geology and wildlife (all protected) in the area, and provides maps of hiking and bicycle trails and details of picnic sites. Park rangers are also on hand to give advice. Climbing should be undertaken only by experts with the correct equipment. Stick to the trails and be aware of weather conditions—flash floods do occur.

**Loop the loop** The 13-mile (21km) one-way Scenic Drive, leaving from the Visitor Center, lets you see some of the best rock formations and take photos at the Calico Vista viewpoints.

## THE BASICS

redrockcanyonlv.org

✚ See map ▷ 108

✉ 20 miles (32km) west of Las Vegas

☎ Red Rock Visitor Center: 702/515-5367

🕐 Red Rock Canyon Visitor Center: daily 8–4.30; Scenic Drive: Nov–Feb daily 6am–5pm, Mar & Oct 6am–7pm, Apr–Sep 6am–8pm

♿ Few

🅿 Parking: inexpensive; free for hikers. Scenic Drive: inexpensive

## HIGHLIGHTS

- Sharks up to 9ft (2.75m) in length
- Underwater Tunnel
- Rare Komodo dragon
- Touch Pool
- Golden crocodiles

## TIP

- Naturalist staff are available around the pathways to help answer your questions.

Fifteen different species of shark, plus 85 other magnificent aquatic species can be encountered close up in the imaginatively re-created marine environments of this excellent aquarium.

**Massive tanks** Shark Reef covers more than 95,000sq ft (8,825sq m) and its tanks—arranged in 14 main exhibits—contain an incredible 1.6 million gallons (6 million liters) of mineral-rich reconstituted sea water. It is home to more than 2,000 marine creatures—not only the 100 or so sharks, but also sea turtles, reptiles, and fish.

**The major exhibits** In Shipwreck Exhibit, a sunken ship sits on the bed of a lagoon, circled by seven kinds of shark. Shoals of snapper and

Clockwise from far left: Walking through the impressive Reef Tunnel; getting up close and personal in the Touch Pool; a sandtiger shark; a rare shark ray; the golden crocodile is a hybrid of a saltwater and Siamese crocodile

jack dart around, in contrast to the laidback gliding of the green sea turtles. The exciting experience of diving on a coral reef is cleverly recreated in the walk-through underwater tunnel, whose water is full of bright tropical fish to the left, right and above you. There is every probability of coming nose to nose with gray reef sharks. Elsewhere, you will see rays skimming through the water or resting on the "ocean" floor.

**Reptiles, amphibians and jungle flora** Rare golden crocodiles can be found in the Crocodile Habitat (one of the few places in the western hemisphere where you can see them), and a rare Komodo dragon is close by. In the Touch Pool you can get hands-on with stingrays and the prehistoric-looking horseshoe crabs.

### THE BASICS

sharkreef.com
🚹 C11
✉ Mandalay Bay, 3950 Las Vegas Boulevard South
☎ 702/632-4555
🕐 Sun–Thu 10–8, Fri–Sat 10–10
🍴 Cafés and restaurants at Mandalay Bay
🚇 MGM Grand
🚌 Deuce, SDX
♿ Very good
💲 Moderate

### HIGHLIGHTS

● The Grand Lobby
● Carillon art-deco bell tower

### TIP

● There are free guided tours Mon and Sat 10am and noon (advance online booking required).

The sophisticated showpiece of Downtown's ongoing revitalization, this magnificent complex offers a world-class program of live performance of music, drama and dance.

**Classic style, dynamic content** The Smith Center for the Performing Arts comprises three theaters, and is the home of the Nevada Ballet Theatre and Las Vegas Philharmonic Orchestra. The complex is topped by a huge art-deco bell tower. Its largest theater is the 2,050-seat Reynolds Hall, with an orchestra pit that can hold up to 100 musicians. There is also the 250-seat Cabaret Jazz club; the 250-seat Troesh Studio Theater; and the Donald W. Reynolds Symphony Park, for outdoor concerts. Its formal hub is the Grand Lobby, a spectacular space decorated with chandeliers and artworks.

*Clockwise from far left: The Carillon Tower and the eye-catching Pipe Dream Sculpture; looking down the grand central staircase; ballerinas practicing in the dance hall; state-of-the-art Reynolds Hall*

**High artistic aims** The center's mandate is to provide a weekly program of entertainment, spanning classical, jazz, country and rock music, as well as ballet and modern dance. Global stars have included Yo-Yo Ma, Burt Bacharach and Dianne Reeves. Its Broadway hit series has featured critically acclaimed shows such as *The Phantom of the Opera* and *Motown: The Musical*.

**Local roots** The Smith Center is equally committed to providing an arts platform and educational facility for the local community. It is one of the partners of the Any Given Child program, which provides a long-term arts education for students in Southern Nevada. It is also the home for the DISCOVERY Children's Museum (▷ 67).

### THE BASICS

thesmithcenter.com
🔒 F3
✉ 361 Symphony Park Avenue
☎ 702/749-2000 (box office)
🕐 Mon–Sat 10–6 (box office)
🍴 Several bars and snack counters
🚇 Several, including SDX and WAX, then a 5-minute walk
♿ Very good
💰 Expensive

## HIGHLIGHTS

● The view from the observation deck
● A gourmet meal in the Top of the World restaurant
● The thrill rides

If zooming up the tallest free-standing observation tower in the United States isn't exciting enough for you, the highest thrill rides in the world await you at the top, along with a revolving gourmet restaurant and breathtaking views.

**On top of the world** Marking the northern end of The Strip, the Stratosphere stands in the shadow of its 1,149ft (350m) tower, which is the main attraction. By means of speedy double-decker elevators, you can be at the five-floor complex known as the pod, which starts at 832ft (254m), in less than 40 seconds and enjoy spectacular views from the indoor observation lounge or the open-air deck. Beneath this is the revolving Top of the World gourmet restaurant (▷ 149).

## THE BASICS

stratospherehotel.com

✚ E5–F5

✉ 2000 Las Vegas Boulevard South

☎ 702/380-7777

🎡 Rides: Sun–Thu 10am–1am, Fri–Sat 10am–2am

🍴 Top of the World restaurant; casino and restaurants $–$$$

🚇 SLS Las Vegas

🚌 Deuce, SDX

♿ Very good

🎟 Tower: moderate (no charge if you have a restaurant reservation); Individual rides, including admission to tower: moderate; Multiride ticket: expensive

❓ You must be at least 48in (1.22m) tall to ride the Big Shot, and 52in (1.32m) to ride X-Scream and Insanity

**High-level thrills, low-level fun** Attractions at the top of the tower are not for anyone who suffers from vertigo. Big Shot, 921ft (281m) high, propels you upward at 45mph (72kph), creating a G-force of four, then plummets at zero gravity. X-Scream dangles you off the side of the building, shooting you out in a small car 27ft (8m) over the edge of the tower, some 866ft (264m) above the ground. Insanity, the ultimate in thrill rides, lets you experience centrifugal forces of three Gs while being spun 64ft (20m) beyond the edge of the tower, 900ft (274m) up. SkyJump is an 855ft (261m) jump from the tower, shooting down a wire cable at high speed, then touching down gently on a landing pad. Alternatively, visit the AirBar, more than 800ft (244m) above The Strip, for cocktails with panoramic views.

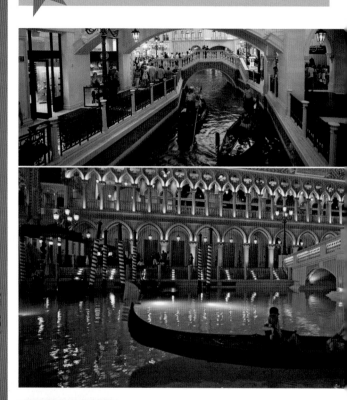

### HIGHLIGHTS

● St. Mark's Square
● Grand Canal
● Street entertainers
● Grand Canal Shoppes
● Madame Tussauds

### TIPS

● Reservations for gondola rides can only be made in person on the same day.
● You will have to walk a lot to see the whole complex; wear comfortable walking shoes.

The Strip's very own replica of Venice has gone a long way to catch the flavor of this most romantic city. But at the same time it has all the glitz and pizzazz expected from Las Vegas.

**Most authentic** This $1.5 billion resort is one of the city's most aesthetically pleasing properties. The ornate lobby has domed and vaulted ceilings, exquisite marble floors and reproductions of frescoes framed in gold. An excellent take on Venice, it has its own 1,200ft-long (366m) Grand Canal—the real one extends 2.5 miles (4km). The waterway meanders under arched bridges, including the Rialto, and past the vibrant piazza of St. Mark's Square where living statues amaze kids with their immovable poses. Replica works of artists

Clockwise from far left: A replica of Venice's Grand Canal runs past the Grand Canal Shoppes; a café on a replica of St. Mark's Square; The Venetian at night; frescoes adorn the ceiling of the casino; gondola ride on a replica of the Grand Canal

Tiepolo, Tintoretto and Titian hang in the casino. The Venetian is also home to Madame Tussauds interactive wax museum (▷ 32–33).

**Gondola ride** From St. Mark's, you can board a gondola and be carried down the Grand Canal to the soothing sound of water lapping against the sides; there is even a wedding gondola. Everything looks particularly spectacular at dusk, when the spirit of Venice is best captured.

**Time to shop** The Grand Canal Shoppes mall (▷ 119) lines an indoor cobblestoned plaza alongside the canal and is linked by walkways. There are fine restaurants and interesting shops behind faux facades, where strolling opera singers perform Italian arias and various other street entertainers do their thing.

## THE BASICS

venetian.com

✚ D8

✉ 3355 Las Vegas Boulevard South

☎ 702/414-1000. Grand Canal Shoppes/gondola ride: 702/414-4525

🕐 Gondola ride: indoor Sun–Thu 10am–11pm, Fri–Sat 10am–midnight; outdoor: daily 11–10; last ride 15 min before closing

🍴 Several cafés and restaurants $–$$$

🚉 Harrah's/The LINQ

🚌 Deuce

♿ Very good

💰 Gondola ride: expensive

## HIGHLIGHTS

● Each chapel has a wedding planner for a stress-free ceremony
● Whatever the happy couple visualize can become reality
● Couples can get married any time of day (or night, at some chapels)

Whether your ideal wedding is being married by Elvis, tying the knot in a hot-air balloon, going for the quick drive-through ceremony or just a traditional approach, Vegas will have a chapel that can oblige.

**What your heart desires** Many hotels have elegant wedding chapels, or you can opt for an outdoor location amid majestic Nevada mountains and canyons. Anything goes in Las Vegas. If you're going to the chapel and you're going to get married, then the chapels lined up along Las Vegas Boulevard north of Sahara Avenue will provide a day to remember.

**Gathered together in the sight of Elvis** The Graceland Wedding Chapel and Viva Las Vegas Wedding Chapel offer the most renowned style

*Clockwise from far left: Just one of the wedding themes on offer at the Viva Las Vegas Wedding Chapels; the Little White Wedding Chapel; an Elvis lookalike sings at a wedding; rent a stretch limo and arrive in style; Viva Las Vegas Wedding Chapel's famous pink Cadillac*

of wedding in Las Vegas, the one that's conducted by an Elvis lookalike. Graceland (▷ 70) is small, offering a more intimate experience, while Viva Las Vegas has options, such as riding into the chapel in a pink Cadillac.

**Chapel of the Bells** Follow in the footsteps of TV personality Kelly Ripa and soccer legend Pelé in this intimate, old-fashioned venue. Among their promotions are a candlelight ceremony and personalized wedding certificate.

**Little White Wedding Chapel** The setting of many celebrity weddings, the chapel is famous for its traditional ceremonies that run until after midnight—simply show up and wait your turn. The drive-through Tunnel of Love has a ceiling with painted cherubs.

---

**THE BASICS**

**Viva Las Vegas Wedding Chapels**
vivalasvegasweddings.com
➕ F4
✉ 1205 Las Vegas Boulevard South
☎ 702/384-0771

**Chapel of the Bells**
chapelofthebells
lasvegas.com
➕ F5
✉ 2233 Las Vegas Boulevard South
☎ 702/735-6803

**Little White Wedding Chapel**
alittlewhitechapel.com
➕ F4
✉ 1301 Las Vegas Boulevard South
☎ 702/382-5943

### HIGHLIGHTS

- Waterfall and lagoon
- Lake of Dreams show
- Art collection
- Le Rêve show

This $2.7 billion resort opened in 2005, a stunning creation by Las Vegas entrepreneur and developer Steve Wynn. If you can't afford to stay here, there's nothing to stop you gazing at its magnificence.

**Dazzling splendor** This incredible showpiece covers 215 acres (87ha) and is one of the tallest buildings in Vegas, towering 50 stories over The Strip. The grounds are an evergreen oasis with trickling streams, the scent of fresh flowers and an integrated 18-hole golf course (open to guests only).

**Spectacles for free** A lagoon backed by a 150ft (46m) artificial mountain, complete with a 40ft-high (12m) waterfall, takes center stage. A visual spectacular, the Lake of Dreams, is

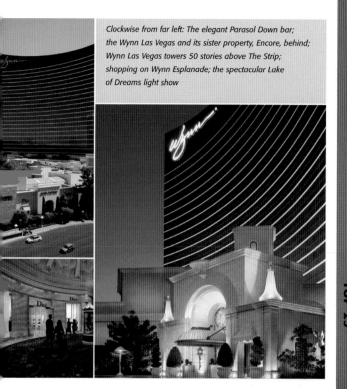

*Clockwise from far left: The elegant Parasol Down bar; the Wynn Las Vegas and its sister property, Encore, behind; Wynn Las Vegas towers 50 stories above The Strip; shopping on Wynn Esplanade; the spectacular Lake of Dreams light show*

projected onto the water and a screen that rises out of the lagoon. Window-shop on Wynn Esplanade (▷ 123), with its collection of designer shops, including famous European designers such as Prada, Dior, Givenchy, Louis Vuitton and Chanel. Steve Wynn's personal art collection is kept here too, in the executive offices; it includes works by Matisse, Renoir and Rembrandt.

**Sensational performance** For a memorable experience, try not to miss Le Rêve—an aquatic show in an aqua theater-in-the-round that dazzles with its extraordinary acrobatic feats, amazing sound-and-light effects and superb choreography. The show is named for a Picasso painting formerly owned by Wynn but sold in 2013 for a reported $155 million.

### THE BASICS

wynnlasvegas.com
✚ D7–E7
✉ 3131 Las Vegas Boulevard South
☎ 702/770-7000
🕐 Lake of Dreams: shows nightly every half hour, dusk to 11.30pm; Le Rêve: Fri–Tue 7 and 9.30pm
🍴 Several restaurants and cafés $–$$$$
🚉 Harrah's/The LINQ
🚌 Deuce, SDX
♿ Very good
💧 Waterfall show: free; Le Rêve: very expensive

# More to See

This section contains other great places to visit if you have more time. Some are in the heart of the city while others are a short journey away, found under Farther Afield. This chapter also has fantastic excursions that you should set aside a whole day to visit.

MORE TO SEE

# In the Heart of the City

### THE ARTS FACTORY

theartsfactory.com

At this complex in Downtown's 18b Las Vegas Arts District, talented local artists are showcased across some 25 galleries and studios. This is one of the main venues for First Friday events, which are held on the first Friday of each month. Galleries stay open late (6–10pm), artists display their work and street bands perform.

🔼 F4 ✉ 107 East Charleston Boulevard ☎ 702/383-3133 ⏰ Gallery and studio opening times vary; some areas are closed to the public; Barbistro: Sun 11–8, Mon–Thu 11–10, Fri–Sat 11am–midnight 🚌 Deuce, SDX 🎫 Free

### THE AUTO COLLECTIONS

autocollections.com

Located on the fifth level of a casino parking garage, a huge showroom displays a collection of 250 classic and special-interest cars, spanning a century of motoring. Some of the vehicles holding the greatest fascination were once owned by celebrities. All of the exhibits are for sale.

🔼 D8–D9 ✉ The LINQ, 3535 Las Vegas Boulevard South ☎ 702/794-3174 ⏰ Mon–Sat 10–5 🚌 Harrah's/The LINQ 🎫 Moderate

### CANYON RANCH SPACLUB

canyonranch.com

At this deluxe spa, the theme is bliss through aquathermal rejuvenation—take your pick of a Finnish sauna, crystal steam room, a multisensory rain room, a herbal laconium, and more. A full menu of spa treatments and a state-of-the-art fitness center with group classes are available, too.

🔼 D8 ✉ Grand Canal Shoppes, The Venetian, 3355 Las Vegas Boulevard South ☎ 702/414-3600 ⏰ Daily 6–8 🍴 Café and restaurant 🚌 Deuce 🎫 Very expensive

### CARROLL SHELBY MUSEUM

shelby.com

Part classic car museum, part auto dealership, this stop south of The Strip, near the Town Square mall, was created by legendary auto race car driver and auto designer Carroll Shelby, who helped mold

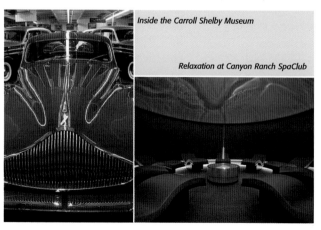

*Inside the Carroll Shelby Museum*

*Relaxation at Canyon Ranch SpaClub*

the Cobra and Mustang models. Take a free 90-minute guided factory tour, or browse the showroom and gift shop.

🏳 Off map at D12 ✉ 6405 Ensworth Street ☎ 702/942-7325 🕐 Mon–Sat 9.30–6, Sun 10–4; guided tours at 10.30am Mon–Sat, 1.30pm Mon–Fri 🚍 SDX
💷 Admission and tours free

## CIRCUS CIRCUS

circuscircus.com

Step inside the Big Top to find aerialists, acrobats, jugglers and clowns performing for free above the casino floor. This is one of the most family-friendly resorts, with a high-speed roller coaster and other thrills in the Adventuredome.

🏳 E6 ✉ 2880 Las Vegas Boulevard South ☎ 702/794-3939 🕐 Adventuredome: Sun–Thu 10–9, Fri–Sat 10am–midnight 🚋 SLS Las Vegas 🚍 Deuce
💷 Adventuredome: all-day pass expensive; individual rides inexpensive–moderate

## CSI: THE EXPERIENCE

lasvegas.csiexhibit.com

Based on the hit TV series, here you can choose from four grisly crimes and follow clues in reconstructed scenes, which include forensic science labs, to discover if you make the grade as a sleuth.

🏳 D10 ✉ MGM Grand, 3799 Las Vegas Boulevard South ☎ 702/531-3826 🕐 Daily 9–9 🚋 MGM Grand 🚍 Deuce, SDX 💷 Expensive

## DISCOVERY CHILDREN'S MUSEUM

discoverykidslv.org

Constantly changing exhibits introduce children to the wonders of science, communication technology and the environment. It's lots of fun, with interactive, hands-on activities, and should appeal particularly to under-5s. There are also themed displays, and fun experiments to try out. The museum inhabits a large three-story building next to the Smith Center, in Symphony Park.

🏳 F3 ✉ 360 Promenade Place ☎ 702/382-3445 🕐 Jun–Aug, Mon–Sat 10–5, Sun 12–5; Sep–May Tue–Fri 9–4, Sat 10–5, Sun 12–5 🍴 Café Dino-Mite 🚍 SDX
💷 Moderate

*Get into character at CSI: The Experience*

*The vertical drop ride at Circus Circus*

## ENCORE BEACH CLUB

encorebeachclub.com

Dress to impress at The Strip's hottest pool party, where world-famous DJs like David Guetta and Diplo spin dance music for a sexy, young crowd. Book ahead for VIP service that lets you luxuriate in a private cabana, daybed, lounger or even on an artificial lily pad.

🚼 E7 ✉ Encore Las Vegas, 3121 Las Vegas Boulevard South ☎ 702/770-7300 🕐 Fri, Sun 11–7, Sat 10–7 Mar–Sep only 🚌 Deuce, SDX 💲 Expensive–very expensive

## EXCALIBUR

excalibur.com

Cross the drawbridge into this fantasyland to join King Arthur and his knights. Inside you will find costumed performers and one of the most popular dinner shows: the Tournament of Kings.

🚼 D10 ✉ 3850 Las Vegas Boulevard South ☎ 702/597-7600 🕐 Tournament of Kings: Mon, Fri 6pm, Wed–Thu, Sat–Sun 6 and 8.30pm 🚈 MGM Grand 🚌 Deuce, SDX 💲 Admission free; dinner show very expensive

## FASHION SHOW

thefashionshow.com

This mall is one of the country's largest and the city's premier retail destination. It is anchored by eight popular department stores: Macy's (▷ 121), Macy's Men's, Neiman Marcus, Nordstrom, Saks Fifth Avenue, Dillard's, Forever 21 and Dick's Sporting Goods. The structure enclosing the mall, known as the Cloud, acts as shade during the day and a screen at night. Fashion runway shows take place hourly on weekend afternoons.

🚼 D7 ✉ 3200 Las Vegas Boulevard South ☎ 702/369-8382 🕐 Mon–Sat 10–9, Sun 11–7 🍴 Numerous restaurants and cafés 🚈 Harrah's/Imperial Palace 🚌 Deuce

## FOUR SEASONS SPA

fourseasons.com/lasvegas/spa

Come here for the ultimate in luxury pampering. Treatments include facials, body scrubs, and massages, and there are two private spa suites, with sauna, steam room, whirlpool tub and massage table. The fitness center includes cardiovascular equipment

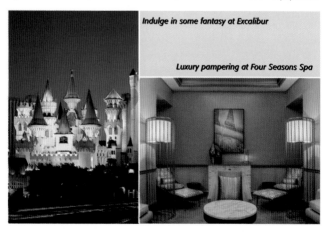

*Indulge in some fantasy at Excalibur*

*Luxury pampering at Four Seasons Spa*

and weights while the spa has saunas and Jacuzzis.

🔳 D11  ✉ Four Seasons, 3960 Las Vegas Boulevard South  ☎ 702/632-5000
🕘 Spa: daily 8–8; Fitness center: daily 6–9
🚌 Deuce, SDX  💰 Very expensive

## GALLERY OF FINE ART

bellagio.com

The first art gallery on The Strip shows a serious side to Las Vegas culture. Inside the Bellagio casino resort, this non-commercial venue showcases two small, but high-quality art exhibitions per year from major museums across the US and beyond.

🔳 D9  ✉ Bellagio, 3600 Las Vegas Boulevard South  ☎ 702/693-7871
🕘 Daily 10–8, last admission 30 minutes before closing  🚌 Deuce, SDX
💰 Moderate

## GAMEWORKS

gameworks.com

GameWorks is the ultimate in interactive, virtual-reality arcade games. It is geared mostly to teens, although any visitor under 18 years must be accompanied by an adult (over 21) after 9pm. Located south of The Strip, it features a 225-seat restaurant, plus 125 video games, a sports bar with screens, a bowling alley, pool tables, and eSports Gaming Center for multiplayer games.

🔳 Off map at D12  ✉ Town Square 6587 Las Vegas Boulevard South  ☎ 702/978-4263  🕘 Sun–Thu 11am–midnight, Fri–Sat 11am–1am  🚌 Deuce, SDX
💰 Admission free; individual activities inexpensive–moderate

## GOLDEN NUGGET

goldennugget.com

One of Las Vegas' original casinos, the glittering Golden Nugget was built in 1946. The star attraction is The Tank—a central water feature complete with a huge 200,000-gallon (757,082-liter) shark tank. Hotel guests can slide down a transparent tube through the middle of the tank to get a closer view of its residents.

🔳 G3  ✉ 129 Fremont Street
☎ 702/385-7111  🕘 Daily 24 hours. Tank viewing area: daily 10–10  🚌 Deuce, SDX  💰 Free

*The Golden Nugget, one of Las Vegas' oldest casinos*

## GRACELAND WEDDING CHAPEL

gracelandchapel.com

Graceland has been marrying couples for more than 50 years, and is one of the many Elvis "shrines," where the bride and groom can take their vows before a lookalike of the King himself. Unless there is a wedding ceremony going on, you can look around the quaint little white-painted chapel, unmissable with its typically Vegas neon sign.

➕ G4 ✉ 619 Las Vegas Boulevard South ☎ 702/382-0091 🕐 Daily 9am–11pm 🚌 Deuce, SDX 💷 Weddings very expensive

## THE GUN STORE

thegunstorelasvegas.com

Ever wanted to fire off an M16 semi-automatic rifle, a Glock pistol, or a double-barreled shotgun? At this shooting range you can, and spend an hour or two pretending to be a Hollywood action hero.

➕ Off map at H10 ✉ 2900 East Tropicana Avenue ☎ 702/454-1110 🕐 Daily 9–6.30 🚌 201 💷 Very expensive

## HOLLYWOOD CARS MUSEUM

hollywoodcarsmuseum.com

Nearly 100 original automobiles and replicas used in Hollywood TV and movies are on display at this warehouse-sized space west of The Strip. Stop by to snap a photo of one of the classic American muscle cars driven in *The Fast and The Furious* movies, a James Bond submarine car, a Batmobile, or the A-Team van.

➕ C11 ✉ 5115 Dean Martin Drive ☎ 702/331-6400 🕐 Daily 10–5 🚌 201 💷 Moderate

## LAS VEGAS NATURAL HISTORY MUSEUM

lvnhm.org

Fun for families, this terrific museum provides a welcome contrast to the high life and glitz of the casinos. There are lots of interactive displays for kids, wildlife exhibits, live animals, animatronic dinosaurs, a replica Egyptian mummy and much more.

➕ H2 ✉ 900 North Las Vegas Boulevard ☎ 702/384-3466 🕐 Daily 9–4 🚌 113 💷 Moderate

*Visitors at Graceland Wedding Chapel*

## M&M'S WORLD

mmsworld.com

An interactive retail complex over four floors with M&M's brand merchandise items, plus a 3-D movie theater, an M&M's Racing team store, and a wall covered in plain and peanut M&Ms.

🚩 D10 ⊠ Showcase Mall, 3785 Las Vegas Boulevard South ☎ 702/740-2504 🕑 Daily 9am–midnight 🚊 MGM Grand 🚌 Deuce, SDX 🖐 Admission and movie free

## MARJORIE BARRICK MUSEUM

barrickmuseum.unlv.edu

An excellent museum devoted to contemporary art and indigenous cultures of the US Southwest and Mesoamerica from 2000BC.

🚩 G10 ⊠ 4505 South Maryland Parkway ☎ 702/895-3381 🕑 Mon–Fri 9–5 (Thu till 8, Sep–Apr), Sat 12–5 🚌 109, CX 🖐 Free–donation

## MARVEL AVENGERS S.T.A.T.I.O.N.

stationattraction.com

Take a leap into the world of Marvel comic books, movies and TV shows at this immersive and interactive experience that lets kids of all ages imagine training to be an agent after successfully fighting Ultron. Peruse Iron Man's high-tech suit, Captain America's uniform, Hawkeye and Black Widow uniforms and weapons, and the recreated laboratory of Bruce Banner, aka The Hulk.

🚩 D8 ⊠ Treasure Island (TI), 3300 Las Vegas Boulevard South ☎ 702/894-7222 🕑 Daily 10–10, last admission 1 hour before closing 🚌 Deuce 🖐 Expensive

## MINUS5 ICE BAR

minus5experience.com

Don a borrowed parka or fake fur coat, then descend into a bar where absolutely everything— seats, chandeliers, sculptures, even your cocktail glass—is made of ice. It's an amusing novelty, and one of Vegas' many oddball experiences.

🚩 D11 ⊠ The Shoppes at Mandalay Place, 3930 Las Vegas Boulevard South ☎ 702/740-5800 🕑 Sun–Thu 11am–2am, Fri–Sat 11am–3am 🚌 Deuce, SDX 🖐 Moderate–expensive

*Hollywood Cars Museum*

*M&M's World, a tribute to the popular candy*

## OLD LAS VEGAS MORMON FORT

parks.nv.gov/parks/
old-las-vegas-mormon-fort

The first people to settle the area were Mormons, who built a fort here in 1855, at a site now considered "the place where Las Vegas began." The fort has been reconstructed, with one original wall surviving, a story told at the Visitor Center.

➕ H2 ✉ 500 East Washington Avenue ☎ 702/486-3511 🕐 Tue–Sat 8–4.30 🚌 113 💵 Inexpensive

## PINBALL HALL OF FAME

pinballmuseum.org

A short detour east of The Strip, this nonprofit museum in a strip mall fills 10,000sq ft (929 sq m) with retro pinball machines and classic carnival and video arcade games from the 1950s through the 1990s, all lovingly restored and maintained.

➕ H10 ✉ 1610 East Tropicana Avenue ☎ 702/597-2627 🕐 Sun–Thu 11–11, Fri–Sat 11am–midnight 🚌 201 💵 Inexpensive

## POLE POSITION RACEWAY

polepositionraceway.com

If you want a break from the casino scene, head west of the Palms casino to this superb indoor go-karting raceway, where you can floor the gas pedal and zoom around the track at thrilling speeds of up to 45mph. Drivers must be at least 56in (142cm) tall to race in adult karts.

➕ A9 ✉ 4175 South Arville Street ☎ 702/227-7223 🕐 Sun–Thu 11–11, Fri–Sat 11am–midnight 🚌 202 💵 Expensive

## QUA BATHS & SPA

caesars.com/caesars-palace

Indulge yourself at one of The Strip's top luxury spas, complete with artificial snow falling in an ice room, saunas, whirlpool baths, plunge pools, and a Men's Zone offering traditional barber services and facials. Book ahead for all spa services and treatments: choose from a relaxing Hawaiian lomi-lomi, Thai-style massage or a traditional Ayurvedic herbal body wrap and enjoy the expert pampering.

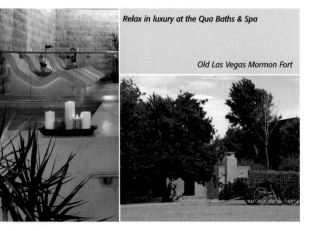

*Relax in luxury at the Qua Baths & Spa*

*Old Las Vegas Mormon Fort*

➕ D8 ✉ Caesars Palace, 3570 Las Vegas Boulevard South ☎ 866/782-0655
🕐 Daily 6–8 🚇 Flamingo/Caesars Palace
🚌 Deuce 💲 Very expensive

## SIEGFRIED & ROY'S SECRET GARDEN AND DOLPHIN HABITAT

miragehabitat.com

Here you can be entertained by marine mammals playing in the lagoon or get up close and personal with some of the rarest and most exotic animals in the world (including rare white lions and white tigers) in a recreated jungle environment, all in one afternoon. Get even closer with exclusive experiences, including a behind-the-scenes VIP tour, "trainer for a day," and other activities such as painting and yoga with the dolphins.

➕ C8 ✉ The Mirage, 3400 Las Vegas Boulevard South ☎ 702/791-7188
🕐 Daily 10–5 (extended hours in summer); last admission 1 hour before closing
🚇 Harrah's/The LINQ 🚌 Deuce 💲 Day pass: expensive; exclusive experiences: very expensive

## SLOTZILLA

vegasexperience.com

This 12-story-high "slot-machine" tower is the launch pad from which riders can shoot up to 1,750ft (533m) down the Fremont Street Experience at speeds of up to 35mph (56kph). There are two adrenline-inducing zip lines: one at 70ft (21m) above street level, or from the upper platform at 114ft (35m).

➕ G3 ✉ 425 Fremont Street ☎ 702/410-678-5780 🕐 Sun–Thu 1pm–1am, Fri–Sat 1pm–2am 🚌 Deuce, SDX 💲 Expensive

## SPA MANDALAY

mandalaybay.com

This opulent facility is a great place to relax, with views over the lagoon and gardens. In addition to all the usual spa treatments, there is a range of more exotic techniques, including a Moroccan hot stone treatment, while other amenities include whirlpools and saunas.

➕ D11 ✉ Mandalay Bay, 3950 Las Vegas Boulevard South ☎ 702/632-4760
🕐 Daily 6am–8.30pm 🚇 MGM Grand
🚌 Deuce, SDX 💲 Very expensive

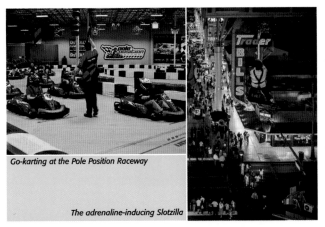

*Go-karting at the Pole Position Raceway*

*The adrenaline-inducing Slotzilla*

### STRIPPER 101

stripper101.com

It's not quite what you might think—instead of being a naughty showgirl revue, this interactive pole-dancing class teaches body positivity for women of all ages, shapes and sizes. No nudity is allowed and you should bring comfy workout clothes and high heels with you.

🔲 D9 ⊠ V Theater, Miracle Mile Shops, 3663 Las Vegas Boulevard South ☎ 866/932-1818 ⊙ Daily (class times vary) 🚌 Deuce ✋ Expensive

### "WELCOME TO FABULOUS LAS VEGAS" SIGN

Designed in 1959 by Betty Willis, this famous sign welcomes you as you enter Las Vegas at the south end of The Strip. On a lawn in the central freeway, the diamond-shaped neon sign is a popular photo stop on guided city tours, often with showgirls and Elvis look-alikes on hand for cheesy portraits.

🔲 D12 ⊠ 5200 Las Vegas Boulevard South 🚌 Deuce , SDX ✋ Free

### WET REPUBLIC

wetrepublic.com

Grab your swimwear and visit the MGM to enjoy two state-of-the-art saltwater pools, eight individual pools and spas, party cabanas and loungers. DJs spin hot beats and entertainers take the stage, while partygoers dance, schmooze or cool off in the water (minimum age 21).

🔲 D10 ⊠ MGM Grand, 3799 Las Vegas Boulevard South ☎ 702/891-3563 ⊙ Apr–Oct Thu–Mon 11–6 🚃 MGM Grand 🚌 Deuce, SDX ✋ Expensive

### THE WILDLIFE HABITAT

caesars.com/flamingo-las-vegas

A lush 15-acre (6ha) paradise has been recreated at the Flamingo casino hotel to provide a home to more than 300 exotic birds, including flamingos, swans, ducks and penguins. Swing by at 8.30am and 2pm daily to watch the brown pelicans being fed.

🔲 D9 ⊠ Flamingo, 3555 Las Vegas Boulevard South ☎ 702/733-3111 ⊙ Daily dawn–dusk 🚃 Flamingo/Caesars Palace 🚌 Deuce ✋ Free

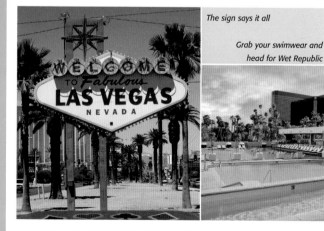

*The sign says it all*

*Grab your swimwear and head for Wet Republic*

# Farther Afield

### CLARK COUNTY MUSEUM

clarkcountynv.gov/parks

Explore Las Vegas' rich and varied past—its Wild West, Atomic Age, Rat Pack and beyond—in this small museum. Complete with a vintage wedding chapel and railway depot, it makes for a quick a stop en route to the Hoover Dam.

➕ See map ▷ 109 ✉ 1830 South Boulder Highway, Henderson ☎ 702/455-7955 🕐 Daily 9–4.30 🚌 HDX
💲 Inexpensive

### CLARK COUNTY WETLANDS PARK

clarkcountynv.gov/parks

Just 9 miles (15km) east of The Strip, this environmentally conscious park has a nature center where you can pick up trail maps and browse exibits. Bird-watching is popular, and species include great blue herons, as well as many varieties of dragonflies.

➕ See map ▷ 109 ✉ 7050 East Wetlands Park Lane ☎ 702/455-7522
🕐 Park: daily dawn–dusk, Nature Center: daily 9–4 🚌 201, then walk 1 mile (1.5km)
💲 Free

### NEVADA STATE MUSEUM

lvnhm.org

This museum provides a welcome contrast to the shows and casinos. There are interactive displays, wildlife exhibits, live animals to pet, animatronic dinosaurs and much more. Just a few of its highlights include a hands-on activity room, whales exhibition, African, marine life and robotic dinosaur galleries.

➕ B3 ✉ 900 North Las Vegas Boulevard ☎ 702/384-3466 🕐 Daily 9–4 🚌 113
💲 Moderate

### SPRINGS PRESERVE

springspreserve.org

Set in 180 acres (73ha) on the site of the original water source for Las Vegas, you can learn more about desert living via interactive displays. There are 110 acres (45ha) of gardens and 3.5 miles (5.6km) trails.

➕ B3 ✉ 333 South Valley View Boulevard, between US95 and Alta Drive ☎ 702/822-7700 🕐 Daily 9–5 🍴 Springs Café Valley
🚌 SDX from Strip north to Downtown, then 207 westbound 💲 Moderate; includes entry to Nevada State Museum

*The delightful gardens at Springs Preserve*

## DEATH VALLEY

nps.gov/deva

The vast Mojave Desert sprawls for nearly 200 miles (320km) west of Las Vegas and heads across the border into North California. It makes for an adventurous day trip, with options for driving tours, hiking and bike rides.

It is the largest national park in the continental US, covering nearly 3.4 million acres (1.4 million ha). It is also the hottest and driest place in North America, with daytime temperatures regularly reaching 120°F (49°C) and rainfall averaging less than 2in (6cm) a year. It comprises a huge range of dramatic landscapes and vegetation: from its highest point at Telescope Peak, 11,049ft (3,368m) above sea level, to Badwater Basin, at 282ft (86m) below sea level—the lowest point in North America. Its geological history has produced a breathtaking array of colored rock layers, carved by erosion over millennia. Some of the best panoramas in the park are at Artist's Palette,

Zabriskie Point, the Devil's Golf Course and Dante's View.

Humans settled here 10,000 years ago, and some of their descendants, the Timbisha Shoshone tribe, still maintain their ancestral homelands in protected areas. Others made their mark more recently, such as Death Valley Scotty, who lent his name to Scotty's Castle, which was built in the 1920s.

Stop by Furnace Creek Visitor Center where you can browse the natural history museum exhibits and pick up free maps and brochures. These give details of hiking trails, as well as guided activities.

**Distance:** 120 miles (193km) northwest of Las Vegas. From Las Vegas take Nevada State Highway 160 via Pahrump to Death Valley junction, then California State Highway 190 to northwest Furnace Creek

**Journey Time:** Over 2 hours

✉ Furnace Creek Visitor Center, California Highway 190 ☎ 760/786-3200 ◉ Park open 24 hours; Visitor Center daily 8–5 ⛏ Moderate

**Pink Jeep Tours**

☎ 702/895-6777; pinkjeeptourslasvegas.com

*Hiking in Death Valley*

*Death Valley is the hottest and driest national park in the US*

## GRAND CANYON

nps.gov/grca

To stand on the rim of the Grand Canyon and look down to its floor below is to be confronted with raw nature at its most awe-inspiring. It's a sight that is timeless, and of which you can never tire.

The Grand Canyon stretches some 277 miles (446km) along the Colorado River, and it is this mighty river that created it, eroding the landscape over 5 million years. This erosion has revealed layer upon twisted layer of limestone, sandstone and shale, a fascinating geological cross-section of the earth's crust. At its widest point, the canyon is 18 miles (29km) from one side to the other and its deepest point is 1 mile (1.6km) beneath the rim.

The South Rim, 275 miles (443km) from Las Vegas, is the more touristy side of the canyon, because it's more accessible, with a rail depot and nearby airport. Grand Canyon Village here has lots of visitor facilities, including hotels, restaurants, shops and museums.

In addition, this is a start point for treks down into the canyon; if you have the energy, this is a wonderful way to appreciate the topography to the full.

More accessible from Vegas, only 125 miles (201km) away, is Grand Canyon West, with its famous Skywalk. The five-layered glass platform, suspended above the canyon floor, offers amazing, heart-pounding views, from 4,000ft (1,219m) up.

**Distance:** South Rim 275 miles (443km) from Las Vegas; Grand Canyon West 125 miles (200km) from Las Vegas
**Journey Time:** 3.5 hours to South Rim; 2.5 hours to Grand Canyon West
✉ South Rim Visitor Center: opposite Mather Point (about 5 miles/8km north of the south entrance station). Grand Canyon West is at the end of Diamond Bar Road, beyond Dolan Springs, off US93, 45 miles (72km) from Hoover Dam 🕐 South Rim Visitor Center: daily 9–4.30 (longer during peak times). Skywalk: Apr–Aug daily 7–7; Sep–Mar 8–6 💰 Skywalk: expensive
❓ It is best to take an organized tour. Many companies offer bus, helicopter and light aircraft trips from Las Vegas

*The glass-bottomed SkyWalk at the West Rim of the Grand Canyon*

*Looking out over the canyon from the South Rim*

## MOUNT CHARLESTON

fs.usda.gov/htnf

Only a short drive away and always cooler than Las Vegas—by as much as 40°F (22°C)—this lovely alpine wilderness is a joy to visit.

Located in the forested Spring Mountains, some 40 miles (65km) northwest of Las Vegas, Charleston's peak reaches 11,916ft (3,632m). It is snowcapped for more than half the year, and is sometimes even visible from The Strip. It lies within the Spring Mountains National Recreation Area, which forms part of the surrounding Humboldt-Toiyabe National Forest. Mount Charleston and its surrounding countryside are popular for their plentiful activities, including hiking (51 miles/82km of trails), horseback riding, mountain biking, rock climbing, picnicking and camping. During winter months, the US Forest Service runs various organized activities, including guided snow-shoe hikes during the weekends. There are campsites with full facilities, as well as picnic areas with hookups for RVs (caravans) and trailers.

Nearby Lee Canyon is a great spot for winter sports, including cross-country skiing and snow-shoeing. Bristlecone pines cling to the limestone cliffs, forming an awesome backdrop. The US Forest Service maintains the trails, which are suitable for all abilities. There's skiing, snowboarding and more at the family-friendly Lee Canyon ski resort (leecanyonlv.com).

At the top of Kyle Canyon, Mt. Charleston Lodge offers homely comfortable log-cabin accommodation, good food and live entertainment in front of an open fire, with breathtaking views (mtcharlestonlodge.com).

**Distance:** 40 miles (65km) northwest of Las Vegas

**Journey Time:** 45 min

☎ 702/515-5400 🛈 Take an organized tour or go by car (check road conditions in winter). From Las Vegas, take the I-15 free-way northbound and continue to US95 north. Stay on US95 until Kyle Canyon Road, then follow signs to Mount Charleston

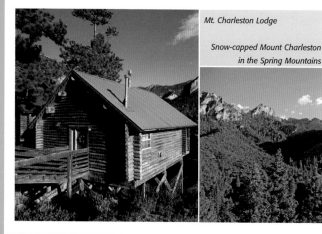

Mt. Charleston Lodge

Snow-capped Mount Charleston in the Spring Mountains

## VALLEY OF FIRE STATE PARK

parks.nv.gov/parks/valley-of-fire

Nevada's first state park takes its name from its red sandstone rock formations, formed more than 150 million years ago by a shift in the earth's crust and eroded by water and wind. The resulting weird and wonderful shapes resemble everything from elephants to pianos. You might also be lucky enough to spot tree stumps that have survived from an ancient 250-million-year-old forest.

Note the ancient rock art (petroglyphs) by the prehistoric Basketmaker people and Early Pueblo farmers, who lived along the Muddy River between 300BC and AD1150. Petroglyphs created by these people can be seen on rocks in several sites dotted around the park, including Atlatl Rock (ask for information at the Visitor Center). Geological highlights include petrified logs, and weird sandstone formations created by erosion from wind and water, some of the best examples of which can be seen at Arch Rock and the Beehives. The varied wildlife includes roadrunners, coyotes, lizards, snakes, antelope, ground squirrels and rare desert tortoises.

You can hike along the park's well-marked trails (pick up a map at the Visitor Center), or enjoy its other activities, such as camping and picnicking. The Visitor Center provides information and trail maps. A short scenic drive from here goes up to Rainbow Vista, a lookout point with views of some of the park's most impressive colored rockscapes.

Not far from the Valley of Fire is Lake Mead (▷ 27), which, with its watersports activities and fishing opportunities, makes a good choice for a day trip.

**Distance:** 55 miles (88km) northeast of Las Vegas

**Journey Time:** 1 hour

✉ Visitor Center: 29450 Valley of Fire Road, Overton ☎ 702/397-2088 🕒 Daily dawn–dusk 🎫 Moderate ❓ Take an organized tour or go by car via the I-15 Freeway northbound from Las Vegas

Rock formation caused by the erosion of wind and water

Petroglyph Canyon is famous for ancient rock art

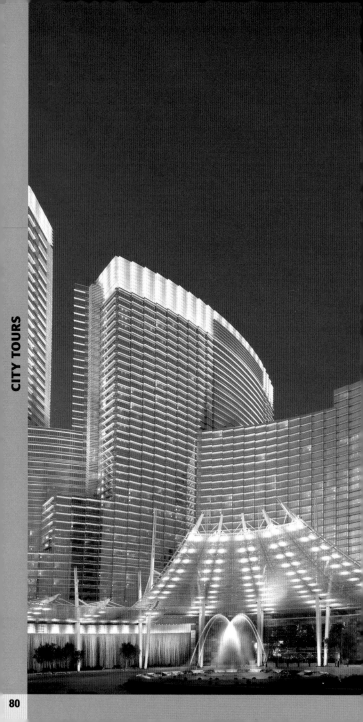

# City Tours

This section contains self-guided tours that will help you explore the sights in each of the city's areas. Each tour is designed to take a day, with a map pinpointing the recommended places along the way. There is a quick reference guide at the end of each tour, listing everything you need in that region, so you know exactly what's close by.

CITY TOURS

# South Strip

Expect a thrilling day of wildlife spectacle, games, and white-knuckle rides. The spacious South Strip also offers some of the city's most adventurous architecture and global cuisine; from New York New York to Luxor and Mandalay Bay, you can eat your way around the world.

### Morning
Start at the Showcase Mall's giant Coca-Cola bottle. Explore **M&M's World** (▷ 71) and join the line at **Tix4Tonight** (▷ 127). Then walk south of MGM Grand, guarded outside by the MGM Lion statue. Inside, cool your heels and splash into the pool party atmosphere at **Wet Republic** (▷ 74), with its cosy cabanas, celebrity DJs and pool.

### Lunch
Cross the walkway over The Strip to **New York New York** (▷ 44–45). Ride the Big Apple around its nearly life-size skyscrapers. Have lunch at **Il Fornaio Panetteria & Restaurant** (▷ 144) Italian bakery and café.

### Afternoon
Cross the walkway over Tropicana Avenue to see **Excalibur's** (▷ 68) medieval fantasy towers. Enter this multicolored castle to visit the Medieval Village. Mingle with costumed performers, dodge the fiery breath of the dragon, and have all sorts of fun exploring the traditional carnival attractions, as well as more up-to-date high-tech games or simulator rides.

### Mid-afternoon

Leaving Excalibur, take a short tram ride down The Strip to **Luxor** (▷ 30–31), one of the city's most striking architectural monuments, fronted by a replica Sphinx. The *Titanic* and *Bodies* exhibitions are an odd combination to find inside a life-size Egyptian pyramid, some might think, but both are hugely popular and moving in different ways. In *Titanic: The Artifact Exhibition*, you can touch a giant block of ice to help you imagine how the passengers might have felt as this huge liner sank, while *Bodies...The Exhibition* shows the inner workings of dissected and preserved human bodies.

### Late afternoon

Take the tram from Luxor down to Mandalay Bay, to visit the **Shark Reef** (▷ 52–53) aquarium inside the convention center behind the hotel. This conservation-oriented feature is arranged in different habitats, with many colorful species of fish and reptiles on show, as well as 15 different species of shark. You can even immerse yourself in the experience, entering an underwater glass tunnel, from which you can watch the fish swimming over and around you.

### Evening

Have dinner at **Fleur** (▷ 142), celebrity chef Hubert Keller's superb gastro-tapas restaurant inside the Mandalay Bay hotel. Soothe your aching limbs at **Spa Mandalay** (▷ 73) and round off your evening with a short taxi ride down The Strip to see the iconic **"Welcome to Fabulous Las Vegas" sign** (▷ 74). The diamond-shaped neon sign standing in the central reservation marks the start of The Strip.

Qua
Baths & Spa

Harrah's
The LINQ

Harrah's/
The LINQ

Westchester
Drive

The Auto
Collections

The LINQ &
High Roller

Ida Avenue

High Roller
Observation
Wheel

Winnick Ave

Caesars Palace &
The Forum Shops

Albert Avenue

EXIT 38

The
Wildlife Habitat

FLAMINGO

BOULEVARD

ROAD

Flamingo

EAST

Flamingo/
Caesars Palace

Gallery of
Fine Art

Bally's

Rochelle Avenue

Bellagio

Paris
Las Vegas

Bally's/
Paris

The Cosmopolitan
of Las Vegas

Miracle Mile Shops

Vdara

Stripper
101

Audrie

Harmon

Harmon Avenue West

Planet
Hollywood

Street

Sinatra Drive

Frank

CityCenter

The
Shops
at Crystals

Signature at
MGM Grand

Aria

Mandarin
Oriental

MGM Grand
Garden Arena

MGM Grand
Conference
Center

Koval Lane

Deckow Lane

Park Avenue West

M&M's World,
Tix 4Tonight

CSI:
The Experience

T-Mobile
Arena

Il Fornaio
Panetteria

Showcase
Mall

MGM
Grand

New York
New York

MGM Grand

Wet Republic

AVENUE

TROPICANA

EXIT 37

Excalibur

Tropicana

Duke Ellington Way

Hollywood
Cars Museum

Reno Avenue West

Reno

Avenue

East

Titanic: The
Artifact Exhibition

Giles Street

Luxor

Pyramid
& Sphinx

Minus5
Ice Bar

Mandalay

Bay

Road

Bethel Ln

Haven Street

Shark Reef

Fleur

Mandalay Bay

Spa Mandalay

Delano
Las Vegas

Four
Seasons
Spa

VEGAS

Four Seasons Drive

I-15

EXIT
36

Mandalay Bay
Convention
Center

Dewey Drive East

Russell Road West

LAS

Bali Hai
Golf Club

0        500 m

0        500 yds

"Welcome to
Fabulous Las Vegas"
sign

C

D

E

National Atomic Testing Museum

Hard Rock Hotel

University of Nevada Las Vegas

Harmon Avenue East

Marjorie Barrick Museum

Naples Drive E

University Road

Thomas & Mack Center

TROPICANA AVENUE EAST

PARADISE

Bell Drive E

Gus Giuffre Drive

Lulu Avenue

Toni Avenue

Laramore Dr
Dalton Drive
De Met Drive
Monika Way

Hacienda Avenue East

Kitty Hawk Way

Westminster Avenue

King Richard Avenue

McCarran International Airport

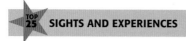
**CITY TOURS**

### Luxor (▷ 30)
Ancient Egypt, the *Titanic* and the human body are all featured here. By night, a laser beam from Luxor's apex shoots high into the sky; it's one of the most memorable sights in Vegas.

### MGM Grand (▷ 34)
Explore this homage to the movie industry; become an instant crime sleuth at CSI: The Experience; or just join the party people at Wet Republic, chilling out in the pool-side cabanas while enjoying the DJ's set.

### New York New York (▷ 44)
Experience the best of the Big Apple at one-third scale, and a sky-high roller coaster. Loop the loop at high speed past the Statue of Liberty, the Empire State Building and the Brooklyn Bridge.

### Shark Reef (▷ 52)
Get up close to an array of sharks, rays and rainbow shoals of colorful tropical fish from inside the glass-walled underwater tunnel at this exciting undersea world. There are experts on hand to explain the mysteries of the deep.

# Center Strip

Have a romantic and visually stunning day exploring the heart of The Strip, combining traditional Vegas razzmatazz with sophisticated contemporary art and architecture.

### Morning

Begin your day at **Paris Las Vegas** (▷ 46–47). Have breakfast in **Mon Ami Gabi** (▷ 146), the only café with tables right on The Strip and great for people-watching over your *café au lait* and *croque-monsieur*. Ride the elevator up the Eiffel Tower for inspiring views all around the city and to the mountains beyond. Look for the thoughtfully placed lens-sized holes in the wire fence on each side of the observation platform, which allow you to take photos unobstructed.

### Lunch

Take a Deuce bus up The Strip, past several casinos, including the Flamingo, to **The Venetian** (▷ 58–59). Go on a gondola ride around the canals, browse the chic shops and have lunch at one of the cafés in St. Mark's Square, serenaded by performing street musicians. Live performances take place at regular intervals, with a timetable posted by the podium in the middle of the square.

### Afternoon

Cross over the walkway to **The Mirage** (▷ 36–37), where you can see the rare animals in **Siegfried & Roy's Secret Garden and Dolphin Habitat** (▷ 73) at the back of the resort. The dolphins are liveliest during feeding and show times, which take place throughout the day, and if you're lucky you might see one of the keepers working with the young white tigers in their enclosure.

### Mid-afternoon

Turn right out of The Mirage and walk through **The Forum Shops at Caesars Palace** (▷ 16–17), with its Romanesque colonnades, talking statues and stylish boutiques. On hot days, cool off in the Garden of the Gods pool area: six open-air swimming pools in manicured gardens decorated with mosaics, marble tiles, rotundas, statues and exclusive cabanas.

### Dinner

Walk south from Caesars Palace and cross the footbridge over Flamingo Road to **Bellagio** (▷ 14–15). Watch the fountain display—every half an hour after dusk—to the music of perhaps Sinatra or Céline Dion. At the hotel, have a buffet dinner, reputedly one of the best in town, or book a lakeside table at **Lago** (▷ 145).

### Evening

After dinner, walk down The Strip to **The Cosmopolitan** (▷ 20–21). Browse the sleek modern tower's super-chic boutiques and lounges by the main entrance. Sip a cocktail in one of its bars draped by the spectacular chandelier, which cascades down several stories in the hotel's atrium. Leaving The Cosmopolitan, walk south for a few more minutes to the stunning **CityCenter** (▷ 18–19) and end the day with more upscale shopping at **The Shops at Crystals** (▷ 122) or in **Aria hotel** (▷ 153), with its casino, bars and lounges, art pieces and sculptures in the lobby.

Meade Avenue

Sirius Avenue

Capella Ave

Stardust

Desert Inn Road W

Desert Inn Road

Sheridan St

Rigel Avenue

Westwood Dr

Highland Drive South

Industrial Road

Polaris Avenue

Procyon Street

Pinks Place

Pollux Avenue

Aldebaran Avenue

EXIT 39

Western Avenue

Fashion Show Drive
**Fashion Show**

Johnny Rockets

**Marvel Avengers S.T.A.T.I.O.N.**

Spring Mountain Road

Treasure Island

The Palaz

**The Mirage**

**Madame Tussauds**

**Siegfried & Roy's Secret Garden and Dolphin Habitat**

**Qua Baths & Spa**

**The Venetia**

BOULEVARD

Harrah's
**The LINQ**

**Rio Convention Center**

Rio

Dean Martin Drive

**The Auto Collections**

**Caesars Palace & The Forum Shops**

EXIT 38

**The LINQ & High Rolle**

**The Wildlife Habitat**

Flamingo Road West

Hotel Rio Drive

FLAMINGO

VEGAS

ROAD EAS

Flamingo

Bally's

**Paris Las Vegas**

Mon Ami Gabi

**Bellagio**

**Gallery of Fine Art**

Polaris Avenue

Aldebaran Avenue

Sinatra Drive

Cavaretta Court

**The Cosmopolitan of Las Vegas**

Vdara

**Miracle Mile Shops**

**Strippe 101**

LAS

Harmon Avenue West

Harmon Avenue West

Frank Sinatra

**CityCenter**

Aria

**The Shops at Crystals**

**Planet Hollywood**

Naples Dr W

**Mandarin Oriental**

MGM Gran Garden Aren

Tompkins Ave W

Rue de Monte Carlo

**M&M's World Tix 4Tonight**

Jerboa St

T-Mobile Arena

**New York New York**

Showcase Mall

**MGM Grand**

TROPICANA AVENUE WEST

Trop Wash

EXIT 37

Tropicana

Reno

Jerboa St

**Hollywood Cars Museum**

Reno Avenue West

**Titanic The Artifact Exhibition**

**Pyramid & Sphinx**

6

7

8

9

10

B

C

D

90

The venturedome

Circus Circus

Elvis Presley Boulevard

(area under development)

THE STRIP

Kismer Drive

(area under development)

(area under development)

Convention Center Drive

Westgate Las Vegas

Westgate Las Vegas Resort & Casino

Joe W Brown Drive

Las Vegas Country Club

bad

West

Channel 8 Drive

Encore Beach Club

Wynn Las Vegas

Wynn Golf and Country Club

Las Vegas Convention Center

Las Vegas Convention Center

Sand

anyon Ranch paClub

Avenue

(area under development)

Country Club Lane

Sierra Vista Drive

Edison Circle

Elm Drive

Royal Crest Cir N

Royal Crest Cir S

Sands Expo & Convention Center

Sands

Avenue

Manhattan Street

Twain Avenue East

rah's/ e LINQ

Westchester Drive

Ida Avenue

Corporate Drive

Royal Crest St

Hazelwood St

gh Roller oservation heel

Winnick Avenue

Albert Avenue

Koval Lane

Howard Hughes Parkway

Center Circle

Hughes Center Drive

Albert Ave

Palo Verde Street

Voxna St

Visby Lane

Northrop Ave

Fredrika Drive

mingo/ sars Palace

FLAMINGO

ROAD

EAST

National Atomic Testing Museum

Bally's/ Paris

Charlotte Drive

Rochelle Avenue East

Hard Rock Hotel

Swenson Street

Harmon Avenue East

Signature at MGM Grand

MGM Grand Conference Center

SI: he Experience

MGM Grand

et Republic

TROPICANA

Koval Lane

Deckow Lane

AVENUE

Monterey Circle

Kelch Drive

EAST

Naples Drive E

Paradise Road

Duke Ellington Way

venue

East

E

0        500 m

0        500 yds

Bell Drive E

Gus Giuffre Drive

F

Palo Verde Road

## SIGHTS AND EXPERIENCES

### Bellagio (▷ 14)
This Tuscan-themed resort takes you to the Italian town on the shores of the scenic Lake Como. Its highlight is the fountain display, with soaring jets beautifully choreographed to music.

### Caesars Palace (▷ 16)
Fountains and Corinthian columns celebrate the glory of Rome. This sumptuous resort is packed with fine restaurants, shopping galleries, a spa and entertainment options.

### CityCenter (▷ 18)
CityCenter is a gleaming architecturally designed complex of luxury hotels, entertainment and retail center, with world-class works of fine art.

### The Cosmopolitan of Las Vegas (▷ 20)
The fashionable Cosmopolitan offers stylish nightlife for the Vegas in-crowd. Don't miss the Marquee club or the bars in the three-story Chandelier.

### National Atomic Testing Museum (▷ 40)
This unique museum traces the evolution of nuclear weapons, beginning after World War II.

### Madame Tussauds (▷ 32)
Wax figures of the world famous come to life in amusing scenes. Popular characters include stars who made it big in Vegas, such as Liberace and the Rat Pack.

### The LINQ and High Roller (▷ 28)
Stroll along The LINQ's outdoor shopping promenade and take a sky-high ride on the world's largest observation wheel.

### The Mirage (▷ 36)
View exotic animals such as lions and tigers in a tropical atmosphere, and marvel at the simulated volcanic eruption in this Polynesian-themed paradise.

### Paris Las Vegas (▷ 46)
The stunningly accurate half-size model of the Eiffel Tower has one of the best views over The Strip. Inside you can experience all the romance of Paris.

### Planet Hollywood and Miracle Mile Shops (▷ 48)
All the glamor of Hollywood is on show in Planet Hollywood, while Miracle Mile Shops offers a relaxed shopping experience.

### The Venetian (▷ 58)
Ride authentic gondolas around the canals in this re-creation of the Italian city. Marbled floors and Renaissance-style artworks adorn the lobbies and shopping arcades.

**CITY TOURS**

CITY TOURS

# North Strip

Have an action-packed day of adrenaline thrills, art and culture in this long stretch of The Strip. Combine walking with hopping on and off the Deuce double-decker bus, using its 24-hour pass.

### Morning

Start your day at **The Arts Factory** (▷ 66), which has the latest in the city's alternative contemporary arts scene. On nearby blocks, you'll find unusual vintage, antiques and souvenir shops, like **Rainbow Feather Dyeing Company** and **Retro Vegas** (▷ 121). Walk east for a couple of blocks along Charleston Boulevard to The Strip and hop on the Deuce bus, passing some of Vegas' most famous **wedding chapels** (▷ 60–61), including **Viva Las Vegas** and the **Little White Wedding Chapel**.

### Mid-morning

Get off the bus at the **Stratosphere Tower** (▷ 56–57). Ride the elevator up and go on the thrill rides, at more than 900ft (275m) above the ground. Its latest daredevil challenge is the SkyJump: the highest controlled freefall in the world, leaping off the edge of the tower attached to a wire. Those with more sedate tastes can simply soak up the highest view in the city from the observation deck. Turn right out of the Stratosphere Tower and walk 10 minutes down The Strip to Sahara Avenue. Along the way, drop in at **Bonanza Gift Shop** (▷ 117), which claims to be the biggest souvenir shop in the world. Over the road, look for the **Chapel of the Bells** (▷ 61), one of the most popular celebrity wedding chapels.

### Lunch

Jump on a Deuce bus and head south to **Circus Circus** (▷ 67). Ride the roller coasters and watch the free circus acts inside the casino in its Adventuredome. Have lunch at one of its many snack eateries, or if you have worked up more of an appetite, gorge yourself at its buffet or on a carnivorous feast at **THE Steak House** (▷ 148).

### Afternoon

Turn right out of Circus Circus and continue walking for 10 minutes down The Strip. Cross over the road to the bronze arc of **Wynn Las Vegas** (▷ 62–63), one of the the most luxurious casino resorts in the city. Explore its marbled halls and exclusive shopping arcades, perhaps indulging in a cocktail or two at the magical **Parasol Down Bar**, which has pretty views over the Lake of Dreams.

### Late afternoon

Crossing back over The Strip, drop into the gigantic **Fashion Show** (▷ 68), for a spot of window-shopping in its glitzy boutiques and department stores. These include the famous **Macy's** (▷ 120).

### Evening

Have dinner at one of the mall's many restaurants, such as the fun and lively fast-food diner **Johnny Rocket's** (▷ 144). Back on The Strip, cross over the elevated walkway again and walk a few minutes north to Wynn Las Vegas to round off your evening at the Encore's **XS** (▷ 135), favored club of the city's well-heeled.

# **North Strip** Quick Reference Guide

**SIGHTS AND EXPERIENCES**

### Stratosphere Tower (▷ 56)

For extra excitement, there are high-adrenaline rides at the top of the tallest free-standing observation tower in the US. From the platform looming more than 800ft (244m) over The Strip, you can challenge your nerves on four different rides, including SkyJump—the highest controlled freefall in the world.

### Wedding chapels (▷ 60)

Getting married in a Las Vegas wedding chapel is an event you will never forget. From driving into a chapel in a pink Cadillac with Elvis at the wheel to getting hitched in a helicopter, anything goes. You can even hire fancy dress costumes of your favorite movie characters to make it the ultimate fantasy experience.

### Wynn Las Vegas (▷ 62)

This luxury resort brims with opulence. It's not just one of the tallest buildings in the city, it also has its own 18-hole golf course, a lagoon backed by an artificial mountain and even a superb collection of original masterpieces on the premises.

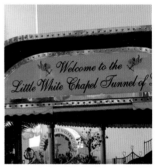

**CITY TOURS**

# Downtown

Discover the city's roots at a new museum dedicated to its shady mafia associations, and an outdoor collection of some of its original neon signs. End your day here after dusk, as a blaze of neon and pounding music fills the Fremont Street Experience's arched roof.

### Morning
Start at El Cortez, the only Downtown property whose exterior has remained mostly unaltered. Walk two blocks west on Fremont Street, crossing over Las Vegas Boulevard, to the Neonopolis Mall. Outside are neon signs salvaged from long-gone Las Vegas landmarks, such as Aladdin's lamp. In the oudoor atrium, the elevator shaft is encircled by vintage neon signs, too. Find even more outdoor displays of classic neon signs by walking two blocks west along the Fremont Street pedestrian mall, then north on 3rd Street. Cross over Stewart Avenue and on the next block is the old post office and federal building—a neoclassical structure built in 1933. Visit **The Mob Museum** (▷ 38–39). This major collection charts the rise and fall of organized crime in Las Vegas, in the former courthouse where a historic hearing marked the beginning of the end of the Mob gangster era.

### Lunch
Continue to the end of Stewart Avenue. At the T-junction with Main Street is **Main Street Station** (▷ 156–157). This is one of the most floridly decorated hotels in Downtown; stained-glass windows and chandeliers add color and sparkle to its casino, and its magnificent bar has a sculpted bronze boar as its centerpiece. Have lunch at the buffet or the brewery restaurant, then pick up a map at the front desk and take a self-guided tour of the art and antiques collection.

### Afternoon
Continue south along Main Street. Two blocks down on the right is the Plaza Hotel, the site of the Union Pacific railroad station, which was once the focal point of Downtown. Cross the road to the Golden Gate, one of the oldest remaining casinos and hotels in the area.

### Mid-afternoon

Turn down Fremont Street under the huge canopy. Look for the neon signs, including **Vegas Vic** and **Vegas Vickie**, part of the open-air section of the **Neon Museum** (▷ 42). Farther down is the **Golden Nugget** (▷ 69), Binion's and the Fremont, three of Downtown's most nostalgic casinos. You'll see people whizzing overhead on the **SlotZilla** zip line (▷ 73), Fremont's Street's latest attraction.

### Evening

Stay for the light-and-sound show of the **Fremont Street Experience** (▷ 24–25), which fills the canopy with a blaze of color (hourly from dusk until midnight or later). Have dinner, either at **Binion's Café** (▷ 140), an economical option inside Binion's, or splash out at **Hugo's Cellar** (▷ 143), in the Four Queens Casino, opposite.

**CITY TOURS**

**SIGHTS AND EXPERIENCES**

### Downtown (▷ 22)
If you're looking for classic Las Vegas, this is the place to find it. Iconic neon signs line the Fremont Street Experience, where you can explore some of the city's casinos.

### Fremont Street Experience (▷ 24)
Be dazzled by this amazing light-and-sound show. Daily at dusk, the arched roof of Fremont Street bursts into life with two million flashing lights and stereo sound.

### The Mob Museum (▷ 38)
Meet the gangsters and the law enforcement officials who finally broke the criminals' control of old Vegas. This museum is based in the original courthouse, the site of some of the showdowns.

### The Neon Museum (▷ 42)
Learn all about the city's fascinating history on a guided tour of this neon sign "boneyard," filled with vintage artworks.

### The Smith Center (▷ 54)
Since opening in 2012, this magnificent arts complex has put Las Vegas on the map, for its superb concert hall and resident orchestra, offering a year-round program of world-class music and drama.

**CITY TOURS**

*Riding Slotzilla's adrenaline-inducing zip lines*

# Farther Afield

On this scenic day's drive out of Las Vegas you can witness the human wonder of the Hoover Dam, then explore Lake Mead on a winding drive around its shoreline, passing harbors, beaches and hiking trails. Arrive at Hoover Dam by 9am, as long lines for the Dam Tour form later in the morning (you can't buy tickets online, although other tours, such as the Powerplant Tour, can be purchased on the official website: usbr.gov/lc/hooverdam).

### Morning
Enjoy the leisurely drive out of the city, heading south-eastward on US93 for 30 miles (48km) to **Hoover Dam** (▷ 26–27). From The Strip, go west to join the I-15 south to the I-215 eastbound, picking up the I-515, which merges with US93, via Henderson after 20 miles (32km). Continue on US93 for 6 miles (10km) to Boulder City, turning left at the second set of traffic lights for another 5 miles (8km) to finally reach the turning onto Nevada State Route 172—the Hoover Dam Access Road.

### Lunch
Continue on NV SR172 for 2 miles (3km) to the Dam. Park in the parking lot in the nearby Visitor Center, and take the guided tour of Hoover Dam. Have lunch afterward at the snack bar near the Visitor Center.

### Afternoon

Leaving Hoover Dam, return along the same road toward Boulder City, turning right after a few miles onto Lakeshore Road (SR 564), the scenic road running along the west side of Lake Mead, part of **Lake Mead National Recreation Area** (▷ 27). Drop in at the Alan Bible Visitor Center, just past the junction, to pick up information about visiting Lake Mead. Drive along the lakeshore, stopping along the way at designated parking spots, from where you can access lakeside paths or take a boat excursion. Continue around the lake; a few miles after leaving the Entrance Station take the second right-hand turn, signposted to Lake Las Vegas Parkway.

### Mid-afternoon

Follow this short road to the **Hilton Lake Las Vegas Resort & Spa** with its picturesque tile-roofed villas and towers, galleries and boutique shops, restaurants and marina.

### Dinner

Dine at the hotel's Medici Café or one of the informal eateries clustered around the cobbled pathways of The Village at Lake Las Vegas.

### Evening

To return to Las Vegas, continue on Lake Las Vegas Parkway, which joins I-515 northbound after about 8 miles (13km), turning right toward the city. Continue for 9 miles (15km) to the junction with Flamingo Road to continue on Lake Las Vegas Parkway back to The Strip. Alternatively, stay the night at the Hilton resort, to enjoy the lakeside tranquility and unwind in the spa and pool.

STATE ROUTE 156

Deer Creek

UNITED STATES HIGHWAY 95

Tule Springs Fossil Beds
National Monument

STATE ROUTE 157
KYLE CANYON ROAD

ORAN K GRAGSON

FREEWAY

RANCHO DRIVE NORTH

Corn Creek Wash

Las Vegas Wash

COUNTY HIGHWAY 21

**Red Rock
Canyon**

CHARLESTON BOULEVARD WEST
**Springs Preserve and
Nevada State Museum**

**LAS
VEGAS**

Flamingo Wash

**McCarran
Int'l**

STATE ROUTE 159

COUNTY HIGHWAY 215

STATE ROUTE 160

STATE ROUTE 160

I-15

LAS VEGAS BOULEVARD

I-215

STATE ROUTE 146

STATE ROUTE 161

LAS VEGAS BOULEVARD SOUTH

I-15

| 0 | | 20 km |
| 0 | | 10 miles |

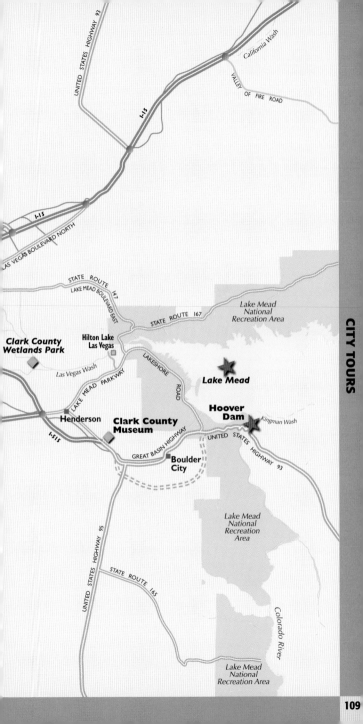

# Farther Afield Quick Reference Guide

**TOP 25** SIGHTS AND EXPERIENCES

### Hoover Dam and Lake Mead (▷ 26)

Less than an hour from the city, the Hoover Dam is one of the world's engineering wonders, and the powerhouse keeping Las Vegas going 24 hours a day. Adjacent Lake Mead, created by the damming of the Colorado River, offers boating, fishing and water-sports.

### Red Rock Canyon (▷ 50)

You'll find these spectacular rock formations only a 30-minute drive from Vegas. The striking layers of red sandstone and green limestone, formed 65 million years ago, contrast with the spiky desert plantlife. Today, the canyon is protected as a National Conservation Area. It forms a great setting for outdoor activities, including hiking, rock climbing and biking.

**CITY TOURS**

| MORE TO SEE | 64 |
|---|---|

Clark County Museum
Clark County Wetlands Park
Nevada State Museum
Springs Preserve

| SHOPPING | 112 |
|---|---|

**Jewelry**
Tiayi Jade Gallery
**Music**
Sam Ash
Zia Records

**Shoes and Accessories**
Las Vegas Chinatown Plaza
Serge's Wigs Shopping Malls
Town Square
**Souvenirs**
Las Vegas Harley-Davidson

**Entertainment and Sports**
Angel Park Golf Club
Las Vegas National Golf Club

Orleans Arena
Royal Links Golf Club

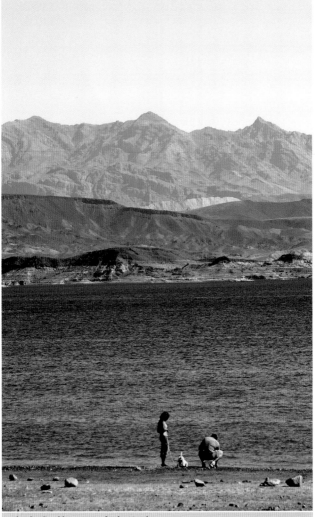

The dazzling blue waters of Lake Mead

CITY TOURS

Dior

# Shop

**Whether you're looking for the best local products, a department store or a quirky boutique, you'll find them all in Las Vegas. In this section shops are listed alphabetically.**

# Introduction

Retail therapy in Vegas has soared in recent years, with an influx of designer stores and hundreds of well-known retailers and flagship department stores that have put the city firmly on the shopping map. Shopping in Vegas mainly revolves around treading the elegant walkways of the numerous malls. As for choice, it depends more on how much money you have to spend and how far you are prepared to travel than on what you are looking to buy.

### A Unique Experience

Most of The Strip hotels have their own shopping opportunities, some more spectacular than others. There is simply no other city in the world where you are able to shop under an artificial sky among Roman architecture and talking statues, or journey between shops by gondola, all within a short distance of each other. Hotel malls in Vegas offer more than just great stores: all sorts of entertainment is lined up to amuse you as you shop, but this is reflected in the cost of the goods. There are other malls on The Strip not attached to any particular hotel, such as the huge Fashion Show (▷ 68).

### Let's Get Serious

Serious shoppers should venture a few blocks away from The Strip, where they will discover

---

**PAWNSHOPS**

The nature of Vegas means there are lots of pawnshops. Many are Downtown and open 24 hours—ready for desperate gamblers to unload their possessions for quick cash. Items that are not reclaimed within 120 days are usually sold. You will discover all sorts of bizarre items at the pawnshops, but jewelry, musical instruments and electrical equipment are the most common. Gone are the days of acquiring items at rock-bottom prices, although you might pick up the odd bargain.

---

*Clockwise from top: The Grand Canal Shoppes at The Venetian line a quarter-mile (400m) indoor canal; luxury shopping at Dior on Via Bellagio;*

less crowded malls that are filled with major retailers and specialist stores selling practical items at more realistic prices. Clothes range from daring and on-trend to boutique exclusives, and the very latest in shoes, lingerie, jewelry and designer glasses complete a look suitable to hit the Vegas scene.

True bargainhunters should head for one of the factory outlets (▷ 120), where top designer clothes, among other things, can be bought at 25 to 75 percent off. Items for the home, electronics and footwear are particularly good value. A lot of the merchandise is end-of-line or last season's. Make sure you are getting top quality and not seconds or damaged goods. Some outlet malls have a shuttle service from hotels on The Strip.

### Souvenirs and Gifts

At the other end of the scale from the classy boutiques are the endless souvenir shops along Las Vegas Boulevard, each selling the same mass-produced card decks and key rings. Every hotel also has a gift shop, with logo merchandise inspired by all the Las Vegas themes, while casino gift shops are generally more elegant and expensive.

**SHOP**

---

#### THAT SPECIAL GIFT

Although Vegas is not known for one particular souvenir—apart from the kitsch in its gift shops—given the time and money, you can buy almost anything here. Gambling merchandise abounds in every guise and quality leather jackets bearing logos are popular. Wine makes a safe gift as Vegas has the largest public collection of fine wines in the world. You might discover that unique collectible you've always wanted—a signed Michael Jordan basketball or autographed Beatles poster. Precious jewels for sale in the city have included Ginger Rogers' engagement ring and the Mogul Mughal (one of the world's largest carved emeralds), but these might break the bank—unless you strike it lucky, of course.

---

*the mosaic-tiled floor on Via Bellagio; get great discounts at Las Vegas North Premium Outlets; Gucci on Via Bellagio; La Scarpa shoe shop on Via Bellagio*

# Directory

## South Strip

**Accessories**
Pearl Moon
**Food and Wine**
M&M's World
**Shopping Malls**
Castle Walk
The Shoppes at Mandalay Place
**Souvenirs**
Houdini's Magic Shop

## Center Strip

**Collectibles**
Field of Dreams
**Fashion**
Carolina Herrera
Fruition Las Vegas
Hard Rock Hotel
Rent the Runway
Tommy Bahama
Versace
**Food and Wine**
Hexx
**Gifts**
Chihuly Bellagio Gallery
**Jewelry**
Le Grand Jewelers
Pearl Factory
**Shopping Malls**
The Cosmopolitan of Las Vegas
The Forum Shops (▷ 16–17)
Grand Canal Shoppes
The LINQ Promenade
Masquerade Village
Miracle Mile (▷ 48–49)
The Shops at Crystals
Via Bellagio

## North Strip

**Department Stores**
Macy's
**Fashion**
Abercrombie & Fitch
Bebe
Forever 21
**Food and Wine**
Teavana

**Shopping Malls**
Wynn Esplanade
**Souvenirs**
Bonanza Gift Shop

## Downtown

**Accessories**
Rainbow Feather Dyeing Company
**Antiques and Collectibles**
Gold & Silver Pawn Shop
Lost Vegas Antiques
Retro Vegas
**Shopping Malls**
Downtown Container Park
Grand Bazaar Shops
Las Vegas North Premium Outlets
**Souvenirs**
Gamblers General Store

## Farther Afield

**Jewelry**
Tiayi Jade Gallery
**Music**
Sam Ash
Zia Records
**Shoes and Accessories**
Serge's Wigs
**Shopping Malls**
Las Vegas Chinatown Plaza
Town Square
**Souvenirs**
Las Vegas Harley-Davidson

SHOP

# Shopping A–Z

### ABERCROMBIE & FITCH
abercrombie.com
Clothing range for young aspiring men and women features the company's stylish preppy-style.
➕ D7 ✉ Fashion Show, 3200 Las Vegas Boulevard South ☎ 702/650-6509
🚌 Deuce, SDX

### BEBE
bebe.com
Sleek designs and curve-hugging wear inspired by the latest trends feature at this sassy boutique.
➕ D7 ✉ Fashion Show, 3200 Las Vegas Boulevard South ☎ 702/892-8083
🚌 Deuce

### BONANZA GIFT SHOP
worldslargestgiftshop.com
The self-styled "largest souvenir store in the world" has a mind-boggling array of tacky mementos. It's worth a visit just to see how tasteless it can all get.
➕ E6 ✉ 2440 Las Vegas Boulevard South
☎ 702-385-7359 🚊 SLS Las Vegas
🚌 Deuce, SDX

### CAROLINA HERRERA
carolinaherrera.com
Dedicated to Herrera's lifestyle collection, this store sells tailored suits, evening wear, cotton shirts and accessories.
➕ C8–D8 ✉ The Forum Shops, Caesars Palace, 3500 Las Vegas Boulevard South
☎ 702/894-5242 🚌 Deuce

### CASTLE WALK
excalibur.com
This mall includes gift shops selling magic tricks, medieval replica swords, shields and even armor.
➕ D10 ✉ Excalibur, 3850 Las Vegas Boulevard South ☎ 702/597-7278
🚌 Deuce

### CHIHULY BELLAGIO GALLERY
chihuly.com
This shop has a good representation of the respected glass sculptor's hand-blown pieces. Chihuly opened his first gallery here, and his biggest sculpture hangs from the Bellagio's lobby ceiling (▷ 14–15).
➕ C9–D9 ✉ Via Fiore, Bellagio, 3600 Las Vegas Boulevard South ☎ 702/693-7995
🚌 Deuce, SDX

### THE COSMOPOLITAN OF LAS VEGAS
cosmopolitanlasvegas.com
Edgy, artful boutiques stock up-to-the-minute fashions, from urban street wear and custom-fitted denim to designer sneakers and swimsuits, all inside this hotel's mini shopping mall. For traffic-stopping diamond jewelry, drop into Jason of Beverly Hills.
➕ D9 ✉ 3708 Las Vegas Boulevard South
☎ 702/698-7000 🚌 Deuce

### DOWNTOWN CONTAINER PARK
downtowncontainerpark.com
Come browse the crafty jewelry, all-natural beauty products and

---

**SHOP**

---

### HOTEL SHOPPING
You will find many familiar stores in hotel malls, such as Gap, Victoria's Secret, Tommy Bahama and Levi's Original, and the classier places will have designer boutiques like Prada and Hermès, too. You won't find the big department stores here, but you'll be able to buy a good range of items, including more mundane requirements such as toiletries, cosmetics and magazines. Souvenirs may include pieces that reflect the hotel's theme, or merchandise from the permanent shows and visiting entertainers.

apparel made by young local designers. This upstart indoor/outdoor shopping mall with bar, restaurants and entertainment is a hub for an arty, young local crowd.

➕ G3 ✉ 707 East Fremont Street ☎ 702/359-9982 🚌 Deuce, SDX

### FIELD OF DREAMS

tristarproductions.com/fieldofdreams
This is the place for sport and celebrity memorabilia, such as a guitar signed by musician Carlos Santana or a jersey autographed by football player Dan Marino.

➕ C8–D8 ✉ The Forum Shops, Caesars Palace, 3500 Las Vegas Boulevard South ☎ 702/792-8233 🚌 Deuce

### FOREVER 21

forever21.com
This department store stocks its own-label of budget casual clothing, accessories and jewelry.

➕ D7 ✉ Fashion Show, 3200 Las Vegas Boulevard South ☎ 702/735-1014 🚌 Deuce, SDX

### FRUITION LAS VEGAS

fruitionlv.com
This ecletic fashion store stocks everything from top designer labels to offbeat vintage apparel, all with an edgy individual flair.

➕ G9 ✉ 4139 South Maryland Parkway ☎ 702/796-4139 🚌 109, 202

### GAMBLERS GENERAL STORE

gamblersgeneralstore.com
What better souvenir of your trip than something with a gambling theme? Take home a roulette wheel, blackjack table, poker chip tray or slot machine. The used-card decks and gambling chips from major casinos are inexpensive.

➕ F3 ✉ 800 South Main Street ☎ 702/382-9903 🚌 108

### GOLD & SILVER PAWN SHOP

gspawn.com
Join the line behind velvet ropes at this Downtown store, made famous by the reality TV series *Pawn Stars*. Filled with art, antiques, collectibles and jewelry, the showroom (where cameras are often filming) is open daily.

➕ G4 ✉ 713 Las Vegas Boulevard South ☎ 702/385-7912 🚌 Deuce, SDX

### GRAND BAZAAR SHOPS

grandbazaarshops.com
This illuminated, canopied outdoor shopping mall shelters an array of accessory, beauty and one-of-a-kind specialty shops. Twice nightly, the two-ton Swarovski Crystal

*The Forum Shops in Caesars Palace*

Starburst dazzles during a free light, video and music show.

🔲 D9 ✉ Bally's Las Vegas, 3635 Las Vegas Boulevard South ☎ 702/736-4988 🚍 Deuce

### GRAND CANAL SHOPPES

grandcanalshoppes.com

This chic Italian-themed mall stretches along a replica of the Venetian Grand Canal and into The Palazzo. Here you'll find more than 100 designers, high-fashion boutiques and Barneys New York department store.

🔲 D8 ✉ The Venetian & The Palazzo, 3377 Las Vegas Boulevard South ☎ 702/414-4500 🚍 Deuce

### LE GRAND JEWELERS

caesars.com/ballys-las-vegas

This upscale store specializes in top-quality pearls, diamonds and gold. Sizing and fitting also offered.

🔲 D9 ✉ Bally's Las Vegas, 3645 Las Vegas Boulevard South ☎ 702/736-7355 🚍 Deuce

### HARD ROCK HOTEL

hardrockhotel.com

An array of boutique and designer shops, including Affliction for tattoo-inspired designs and John Varvatos, a fashionable men's shop that also sells James Trussart custom guitars.

🔲 F9 ✉ 4455 Paradise Road ☎ 702/693-5000 🚍 108

### HEXX

hexxchocolate.com

Nestled at the foot of the Eiffel Tower, this candy store is a sticky wonderland for anyone with a sweet tooth. In addition to all its beautifully packaged bean-to-bar chocolates and candies, it has a brasserie, cocktail bar and exhibition kitchen.

🔲 D9 ✉ Paris Las Vegas, 3655 Las Vegas Boulevard South ☎ 702/331-5551 🚊 Bally's/Paris 🚍 Deuce, SDX

### HOUDINI'S MAGIC SHOP

houdinis.com

Every 15 minutes until midnight you can watch live magic shows, and then buy your own magic tricks from the selection available for sale.

🔲 D10 ✉ New York New York, 3790 Las Vegas Boulevard South ☎ 702/ 314-4674 🚊 MGM Grand 🚍 Deuce

### LAS VEGAS CHINATOWN PLAZA

lvchinatownplaza.com

At this cluster of more than 20 Asian restaurants, shops and food stores, located west of The Strip, you can pick up Asian-style jewelry, clothes, ornaments and Chinese foods. There are also plently of good-value restaurants to choose from.

🔲 A8–B8 ✉ 4255 Spring Mountain Road ☎ 702/221-8448 🚍 203

SHOP

## LAS VEGAS HARLEY-DAVIDSON

lasvegasharleydavidson.com
One of the world's largest Harley stores has a vast array of merchandise and bikes on display for sale and to rent.

🔢 D12  ✉️ 5191 Las Vegas Boulevard South  ☎️ 702/431-8500  🚌 SDX

## LAS VEGAS NORTH PREMIUM OUTLETS

premiumoutlets.com
Save 25 to 75 percent at this large designer and name-brand outlet, whose names include Ann Taylor, Dolce & Gabbana, DKNY, Guess, Calvin Klein, Lacoste, Adidas and Tommy Hilfiger.

🔢 E3–F3  ✉️ 875 South Grand Central Parkway  ☎️ 702/474-7500  🚌 SDX

## THE LINQ PROMENADE

caesars.com/linq
Fun, colorful and casual lifestyle shops line this outdoor walkway just off The Strip. Pick up a pair of collectible sneakers at 12Am Run boutique or print your selfies at Photo & Go.

🔢 D9  ✉️ 3535 Las Vegas Boulevard South  ☎️ 800/634-6441  🚇 Harrah's/The LINQ  🚌 Deuce

## LOST VEGAS ANTIQUES

This colorful little store specializes in vintage Americana dating from Vegas's raunchy era of the Mob, Bugsy Siegel and the Rat Pack. You can browse its wonderful collection of kitsch ornaments, gambling ephemera, movie posters, vinyl records and much more. It's next to the Graceland Wedding Chapel.

🔢 G4  ✉️ 625 Las Vegas Boulevard South  ☎️ 702/382-1882  🚌 Deuce, SDX

## M&M'S WORLD

mmsworld.com
A tourist attraction as well as a candy store and chocolate lover's dream, this place has a huge selection of well-known confectionery brands, including a vast array of liqueur-filled chocolates and, of course, M&Ms.

🔢 D10  ✉️ Showcase Mall, 3785 Las Vegas Boulevard South  ☎️ 702/740-2504  🚇 MGM Grand  🚌 Deuce, SDX

*Come to Mandalay Place for upscale shopping and dining*

## MACY'S

macys.com

The choice at this department store is extensive; all your fashion needs, as well as accessories, shoes and homeware.

➕ D7　✉ Fashion Show, 3200 Las Vegas Boulevard South　☎ 702/731-5111
🚌 Deuce, SDX

## MASQUERADE VILLAGE

Stroll down the tiled streets here to find a range of retail outlets, from candies to original artwork to branded merchandise at the Rio logo store.

➕ B8　✉ Rio, 3700 West Flamingo Road
☎ 702/777-7777　🚌 202

## PEARL FACTORY

See how pearls are cultured before you pick out the ones you like, and have them mounted in the setting of your choice. Hawaiian heirloom jewelry is also displayed.

➕ D8　✉ Grand Canal Shoppes, 3377 Las Vegas Boulevard South　☎ 702/207-0033
🚌 Deuce

## PEARL MOON

It's a bit on the pricey side, but the selection of swimwear, hats, sunglasses and sandals here is better quality than you'll find at other shops on The Strip.

➕ D11　✉ Mandalay Bay, 3950 Las Vegas Boulevard South　☎ 702/632-6120
🚌 Deuce, SDX

## RAINBOW FEATHER DYEING COMPANY

rainbowfeatherco.com

Feathers of every hue and shade are made into boas, ornaments and jewelry, as well as flights for archery. The family of the late master feather-crafter Bill Girard creates accessories, worn by Las Vegas showgirls and Cirque du Soleil acrobats.

➕ F4　✉ 1036 South Main Street
☎ 702-598-0988　🚌 108, Deuce

## RENT THE RUNWAY

renttherunway.com

Browse the latest fashions from New York, Los Angeles, London and Paris at this unique boutique offering same-day rentals for any occasion, from a big night out clubbing to getting married at a Vegas wedding chapel.

➕ D9　✉ The Cosmopolitan of Las Vegas, 3708 Las Vegas Boulevard South
☎ 702/698-7000　🚌 Deuce

## RETRO VEGAS

retro-vegas.com

In Downtown's 18b Arts District, look for pink flamingos out front at this antiques showroom specializing in mid-century modern and vintage art, housewares, jewelry and pocket-sized souvenirs from Las Vegas' "Fabulous Fifties" era.

➕ F4　✉ 1131 South Main Street
☎ 702/384-2700　🚌 108, Deuce, SDX

## SAM ASH

samashmusic.com

Sam Ash is a musicians' playground, stacked high with

SHOP

---

### ARTS AND CRAFTS

Las Vegas has plenty of places where you can buy fine artworks. Classical and contemporary art and sculpture are sold in many shopping malls, including Fashion Show, Forum Shops, Grand Canal Shoppes and other outlets on and off The Strip. The Arts Factory (▷ 66) has many galleries and studios and holds a special monthly late-opening evening.

guitars, amps, drums and brass and wind instruments of every conceivable brand.

➕ H6 ✉ 2747 Maryland Parkway ☎ 702/734-0007 🚌 109

### SERGE'S WIGS

sergeswigs.com

Choose from around 10,000 wigs, in all shapes and shades. Don't be surprised to find a real-life Vegas showgirl shopping beside you.

➕ A6 ✉ 4515 West Sahara Avenue ☎ 702/207-7494 🚌 SX

### THE SHOPPES AT MANDALAY PLACE

www.mandalaybay.com

A dramatic sky bridge connecting Mandalay Bay with Luxor is home to a number of superior retailers. These include top designer names in men's and women's fashion, and renowned jewelry stores, as well as other specialties, bars and casual restaurants.

➕ D11 ✉ Mandalay Bay, 3950 Las Vegas Boulevard South ☎ 702/632-7777 🚌 Deuce, SDX

### THE SHOPS AT CRYSTALS

simon.com/mall/the-shops-at-crystals

Be wowed by the angular architecture of this top-tier mall that seems to jut out into The Strip. Inside are colorfully glowing fountains, a two-story treehouse sculpture and an array of glitzy designer boutiques like Bulgari,

Fendi, Dolce & Gabbana, Jimmy Choo, Tiffany & Co., Tom Ford and Stella McCartney.

➕ D9–D10 ✉ 3720 Las Vegas Boulevard South ☎ 702/590-9299 🚌 Deuce

### TEAVANA

teavana.com

This is tea heaven and an absolute must for all aficionados of the brew. There are white, black and green varieties, plus organic, herbal and many more. The teapots, mugs, storage tins and accessories make ideal gifts for any tea lover.

➕ D7 ✉ Fashion Show, 3200 Las Vegas Boulevard South ☎ 702/369-9732 🚌 Deuce, SDX

### TIAYI JADE GALLERY

This gallery sells an unusual and fascinating selection of high quality, hand-crafted jade jewelry.

➕ A8–B8 ✉ Las Vegas Chinatown Plaza, 4255 Spring Mountain Road ☎ 702/227-9198 🚌 203

### TOMMY BAHAMA

tommybahama.com

If your preferred lifestyle is sitting on the dock of the bay, this is the store for you, with upmarket clothing for men and women, designed for that certain tropical chic look.

➕ C8–D8 ✉ The Forum Shops, Caesars Palace, 3570 Las Vegas Boulevard South ☎ 702/933-6888 🚌 Deuce

## TOWN SQUARE

mytownsquarelasvegas.com
Mediterranean and Spanish-style facades, enhanced by antique streetlights, conceal an eclectic mix of stores, restaurants and bars. A small central park houses a children's playground and picnic area. There is also a cinema.
➕ Off map ✉ 6605 Las Vegas Boulevard South ☎ 702/269-5001 🚌 Deuce, SDX

## VERSACE

versace.com
The late fashion designer's Italian style is obvious in the garments sold here, all made from the finest fabrics. The company's signature lion's head appears on everything.
➕ C8–D8 ✉ The Forum Shops, Caesars Palace, 3500 Las Vegas Boulevard South ☎ 702/932-5757 🚌 Deuce, SDX

## VIA BELLAGIO

This opulent mall has exquisite fashion and jewelry collections from world-renowned designers Chanel, Gucci, Hermès, Louis Vuitton, Prada, Tiffany & Co. and many more.
➕ C9–D9 ✉ Bellagio, 3600 Las Vegas Boulevard South ☎ 702/693-7111 🚌 Deuce

## WYNN ESPLANADE

An endless list of exclusive designer names can be found at this luxury hotel mall. Take your pick from the likes of Alexander McQueen, Cartier, Chanel, Louis Vuitton, Dior, Givenchy, Rolex, Salvatore Ferragamo and other luxury designer brands.
➕ D7–E7 ✉ Wynn Las Vegas, 3131 Las Vegas Boulevard South ☎ 702/770-7000 🚌 Deuce, SDX

## ZIA RECORDS

ziarecords.com
The city's best independent music store is stocked with new and collectible vinyl records, CDs, movie DVDs, graphic novels, video games and books. Check the calendar for in-store celebrity appearances and live shows by bands.
➕ A6 ✉ 4503 West Sahara Avenue ☎ 702/233-4942 🚌 SX

*Bellagio's luxury shopping arcade, Via Bellagio*

# Entertainment

Once you've done with sightseeing for the day, you'll find lots of other great things to do with your time in this chapter, even if all you want to do is relax with a drink. In this section establishments are listed alphabetically.

# Introduction

Vegas really comes alive after the sun goes down, and some of the best attractions are to be found during the twilight hour. Soak up a pulsating nightlife scene like no other—this is a great place to party.

## Endless Variety

From casino lounges to clubs, pubs and cocktail bars, the possibilities for a fun night out are endless. Numerous nightspots provide the chance to dance until dawn. Ultra lounges are the latest trend, stylish spaces that attract a cutting-edge crowd, where DJs spin their vinyl but conversation takes priority. But this is Sin City, and there are several not very well-concealed strip joints scattered throughout. These can, however, be disregarded amid the sheer scale of everything else.

## Only the Best

Las Vegas is infamous for its spectacularly staged extravaganzas, which incorporate unbelievable special effects and have attracted some of the world's hottest superstars. Shows vary from Broadway musicals and spectacular productions to comedy and magic. Vegas also plays host to some of the world's biggest special events, such as world championship boxing matches. The top shows can be expensive and the most popular often need to be reserved well in advance. But the best

### GAMING

Where else could you continually be refueled with free drinks as you play the blackjack table or wait for the roulette wheel to stop spinning? But be careful not to lose it all in one night. If you're not a serious player, the slot machines are lots of fun, too. Strolling through the casinos people-watching is another great way to pass the time—weary gamblers desperately trying to claw back some of their losses, ecstatic cries of joy when their luck holds and the jangling of chips when the slots pay out.

*Clockwise from top: The House of Blues, Mandalay Bay Resort; cocktail bar at Mandalay Bay; the Zebras from the Bellagio's "O"; you can enjoy a cocktail any time;*

show of all is free: walk The Strip after dark and be treated to the amazing performance of thousands of flashing neon lights.

### From Highbrow to Fringe

With the ongoing regeneration of Downtown, a wider range of arts and culture has added to the dazzling spectacle that is The Strip's traditional fare. Opened in mid-2012, The Smith Center is a major new architectural complex, which houses the Nevada Ballet Theatre and Las Vegas Philharmonic. It offers a program of world-class live performances. The fringe music scene is also alive and growing, with open-mike sessions and acoustic gigs at various venues, mostly Downtown in the Fremont East Entertainment District and the 18b Arts District

### Discount Tickets

Top show tickets can cost upward of $100, but you can make big savings at discount agencies and with coupons in the free tourist magazines. Tix4Tonight offers half-price tickets for same-day shows, with kiosks on Mid-Strip at Bally's Grand Bazaar Shops, Planet Hollywood and Casino Royale; also Downtown at the Four Queens on Fremont Street; North Strip at Circus Circus and the Fashion Show; and South Strip at the Showcase Mall next to the giant Coca-Cola bottle. Shows on offer are typically listed at 9.30 daily, with tickets on sale from 10–7 or later, or tel 877/849-4868.

WEIRD AND WACKY

Las Vegas is constantly coming up with increasingly adventurous and sometimes edgy shows. Several hypnosis acts invite volunteers from the audience on stage to commit hilarious acts that border on the lewd. Audience participation is ever popular: take front row seats at your peril. Subtle it ain't, but mainstream shows on The Strip are all about doing it loud and large.

*synchronized swimmers in Bellagio's "O" performance;*
*Le Rêve, Wynn Las Vegas*

# Directory

## South Strip

**Bars, Clubs and Lounges**
Coyote Ugly
Hakkasan
LAX
Skyfall Lounge
**Entertainment and Sports**
Bali Hai Golf Club
House of Blues
Mandalay Bay Events Center
MGM Grand Garden Arena
*Michael Jackson ONE*
The Park
Thomas & Mack Center

## Center Strip

**Bars, Clubs and Lounges**
Cleopatra's Barge
Ghostbar
Gordon-Biersch Brewery
Restaurant
Marquee
Napoleon's Lounge Bar
OMNIA

**Entertainment and Sports**
Absinthe
*The Beatles: LOVE*
Blue Man Group

Brooklyn Bowl
Colosseum
Flamingo Las Vegas
The Joint
Nathan Burton Comedy Magic
Penn & Teller
**Theaters**
UNLV Arts Center
V Theater

## North Strip

**Bars, Clubs and Lounges**
107 SkyLounge
Intrigue
Parasol Down
Peppermill Fireside Lounge
XS
**Entertainment and Sports**
Vegas Indoor Skydiving
Westgate Las Vegas Resort
& Casino

## Farther Afield

**Entertainment and Sports**
Angel Park Golf Club
Las Vegas National Golf Club
Orleans Arena
Royal Links Golf Club

# Entertainment A–Z

### 107 SKY LOUNGE

topoftheworldlv.com
Visit this sophisticated cocktail
lounge bar before or after a meal
at the Top of the World restaurant
(▷ 149). High up on the 107th
floor, it offers a 360-degree view
of the Las Vegas skyline. Martinis
are the house specialty.
➕ E5–F5 ✉ Stratosphere, 2000 Las
Vegas Boulevard South ☎ 702/380-7711
◉ Daily 4pm–4am 🚌 Deuce 🚹 No
cover charge

### ABSINTHE

absinthevegas.com
This thrilling show in-the-round
is highly acclaimed for its jaw-
dropping acrobatics, combined
with equally outrageous burlesque
comedy. In either case, it's not one
for the fainthearted.
➕ C8–D8 ✉ Roman Plaza, Caesars Palace,
3570 Las Vegas Boulevard South
☎ 702/893-4800 ◉ Wed–Sun 8pm and
10pm 🚹 Flamingo/Caesars Palace
🚌 Deuce 🚹 Very expensive

## ANGEL PARK GOLF CLUB

angelpark.com

Experience both mountains and palms at this 36-hole course designed by legendary golfer Arnold Palmer. There are spectacular views over Red Rock Canyon and the Las Vegas Valley.

➕ Off map ✉ 100 South Rampart Boulevard, west of US95 and south of Summerlin Parkway ☎ 888/446-5358 🕐 Daily (opening hours vary) 🚍 WAX 💶 Very expensive

## BALI HAI GOLF CLUB

balihaigolfclub.com

A South Pacific theme runs throughout this 18-hole championship course off the southern end of The Strip, with outcrops of volcanic rock, palm trees and white sand bunkers.

➕ C12–D12 ✉ 5160 Las Vegas Boulevard South ☎ 888/427-6678 🕐 Daily (opening hours vary) 🚍 SDX 💶 Very expensive

## *THE BEATLES: LOVE*

cirquedusoleil.com

Cirque du Soleil's production, *LOVE* celebrates the Beatles' legacy and explores their songs in scenes inhabited by real and imaginary people, all accompanied by acrobatics and dancing.

➕ D8 ✉ The Mirage, 3400 Las Vegas Boulevard South ☎ 702/792-7777 🕐 Thu–Mon 7pm and 9.30pm 🚍 Harrah's/The LINQ 🚍 Deuce 💶 Very expensive

## BLUE MAN GROUP

blueman.com

One of the most unusual shows in Vegas, this group of guys with cobalt-blue bald heads perform hilarious routines, creating artistic canvases by the strangest means.

➕ D11 ✉ Luxor, 3900 Las Vegas Boulevard South ☎ 702/262-4200 🕐 Daily 7pm and 9.30pm 🚍 Deuce 💶 Very expensive

## BROOKLYN BOWL

Nowhere on The Strip will you hear more rockin' indie music than at this hybrid bowling alley, restaurant and concert hall, with nighttime views of the illuminated High Roller wheel.

➕ D9 ✉ The LINQ Promenade, 3545 Las Vegas Boulevard South ☎ 702/862-2695 🕐 Daily 5pm–close (showtimes vary) 🚍 Harrah's/The LINQ 🚍 Deuce 💶 Expensive

## CLEOPATRA'S BARGE

caesarspalace.com

This floating club is a replica of the vessel that carried the Egyptian Queen Cleopatra. A DJ plays dance music during the week, and there's live music on weekends.

➕ C8–D8 ✉ Caesars Palace, 3570 Las Vegas Boulevard South ☎ 702/731-7333 🕐 Tue–Thu 8pm–2am, Fri–Sat 8pm–3am 🚍 Flamingo/Caesars Palace 🚍 Deuce 💶 No cover charge

---

### TICKET INFORMATION

Popular long-running shows and new ones sell out quickly, so it's advisable to make reservations. Call the relevant hotel or check out its website, which will link to online ticket sales. Otherwise, shows can be reserved through TicketMaster (ticket-master.com). Reservations are taken for long-running shows up to 30 or more days in advance; limited-time concerts or sporting events such as boxing matches can be reserved three months in advance. Note that shows can close with little notice so it is always best to check to avoid disappointment.

## COLOSSEUM

caesarspalace.com

This magnificent auditorium has been purpose-built to stage extravaganzas and host international superstars. Céline Dion, Elton John and Mariah Carey are among the star performers.

🔲 C8–D8 ⊠ Caesars Palace, 3570 Las Vegas Boulevard South ☎ 866/227-5938 🕐 Daily (show times vary) 🚍 Deuce

## COYOTE UGLY

coyoteuglysaloon.com/vegas

If you enjoyed the movie or have visited the New York original, you'll love the Las Vegas version. It's a fun Southern-style saloon with bartenders who dance on the bar.

🔲 D10 ⊠ New York New York, 3790 Las Vegas Boulevard South ☎ 702/740-6969 🕐 Daily 6pm–late 🚍 MGM Grand 🚍 Deuce 💵 Cover charge: moderate

## FLAMINGO LAS VEGAS

caesars.com/flamingo-las-vegas

Founded in the 1940s and formerly owned by Mob legend Bugsy Siegel, the Flamingo has long had a high reputation for hosting show business legends— Nat King Cole and Ella Fitzgerald once graced the stage here. Donny and Marie Osmond—still smiling broadly—have been top of the bill. There are also stand-up comedians, magicians and showgirls.

🔲 D9 ⊠ Flamingo, 3555 Las Vegas Boulevard South ☎ 702/777-2782 🕐 Daily (show times vary) 🚍 Flamingo/ Caesars Palace 🚍 Deuce 💵 Very expensive

## GHOSTBAR

palms.com

With its futuristic look, this is one of the city's most talked about bars. You'll find it 55 floors up in the Palms hotel, which means you can marvel at the breathtaking views while music from the DJ fills the background. There's another fantastic view once you are on the outside deck: one looking directly down at the pool below through a glass floor.

🔲 A9 ⊠ Palms, 4321 West Flamingo Road ☎ 702/942-6832 🕐 Daily 8pm– 4am 🚍 202 💵 Cover charge: free–expensive

*Where there's a casino, there's a lounge or bar*

## GORDON BIERSCH BREWERY RESTAURANT

gordonbiersch.com

Exposed pipes and gleaming brewing equipment set the stage for this popular hangout. The beers include seasonally changing German brews.

🔢 F8 ✉ 3987 Paradise Road ☎ 702/312-5247 🕐 Sun–Thu 11am–11pm, Fri–Sat 11am–midnight 🚌 108

## HAKKASAN

hakkasanlv.com

Attached to a double-decker Chinese restaurant, this three-level nightclub offers lounges, fine dining and dancing to the electronic sounds of superstar DJs, including Steve Aoki, Calvin Harris and Tiësto.

🔢 D10 ✉ MGM Grand, 3799 Las Vegas Boulevard South ☎ 702/891-3838 🕐 Wed–Sun 10.30pm–late 🚌 Deuce, SDX 💷 Expensive

## HOUSE OF BLUES

houseofblues.com/lasvegas

Bringing top musical acts to Las Vegas, this 1,500-seat venue is on three levels and features big-name stars, rock tribute bands and DJs in all musical genres. There's great food, including the popular Sunday Gospel Brunch buffet.

🔢 D11 ✉ Mandalay Bay, 3950 Las Vegas Boulevard South ☎ 702/632-7800 🕐 Daily (showtimes vary) 🚌 Deuce, SDX 💷 Expensive–very expensive

## INTRIGUE

intriguevegas.com

One of the most enticing night-clubs in the city, Intrigue sets a new bar for nightlife in Las Vegas. Sophisticated jewel-tone and black combinations enhance intimate booth-style seating and the open-air dance floor extends toward a waterfall that cascades into a lagoon. Dress smartly, no jeans.

🔢 D7–E7 ✉ Wynn Las Vegas, 3131 Las Vegas Boulevard South ☎ 702/770-3000 🕐 Thu–Sat 10.30pm–4am 🚌 Deuce, SDX 💷 Expensive

## THE JOINT

hardrockhotel.com

One of Vegas's hottest venues for live rock music and rap with a capacity of 1,400. The Joint showcases cutting-edge bands worthy of the Hard Rock image, as well as fast-paced sporting events.

🔢 F9 ✉ Hard Rock Hotel, 4455 Paradise Road ☎ 702/693-5222 (box office 10–8) 🕐 Days and showtimes vary 🚌 108 💷 Expensive–very expensive

## LAS VEGAS NATIONAL GOLF CLUB

lasvegasnational.com

Opened in 1961, this 18-hole golf course has glistening lakes. In 1996, Tiger Woods won his first

### DRESS CODES

Most, if not all, of the nightclubs listed here impose quite a strict dress code, so it's a good idea to check what is acceptable beforehand. Men may have more trouble than women when it comes to what they are wearing: jeans and sneakers are guaranteed to keep hopefuls out of any club. You can get onto the VIP list if you know someone who works at the club, or if you have spent a lot in the casino. Otherwise, join the line outside the door (about an hour before opening time at the most popular places) and hope for the best. Cover charges, where they exist, are usually $20–$50.

## CIRQUE DU SOLEIL

This troupe, originally from Québec in Canada, has taken circus arts to new levels with its breathtaking artistic concept shows. It has several shows currently running, including *Mystère* at Treasure Island (Sat–Wed); *"O"* at Bellagio (Wed–Sun); *Zumanity* at New York New York (Fri–Tue); *KÀ* at MGM Grand (Tue–Wed); *The Beatles: LOVE* at The Mirage (▷ 129); and *Michael Jackson ONE* (▷ below). For details browse cirquedusoleil.com.

PGA Tour victory here, and over the years the course has hosted many top-class tournaments.
🚩 J7–J8 ✉ 1911 East Desert Inn Road ☎ 702/889-1000 🕐 Daily (opening hours vary) 🚌 203 💵 Very expensive

### LAX
luxor.com
This huge two-story space with spiral staircases, oversized mirrors and chandeliers, and fabulous decor attracts a young, discerning crowd. Top DJs play from a raised platform through an unrivaled sound system to the packed dance floor below.
🚩 C11–D11 ✉ Luxor, 3900 Las Vegas Boulevard South ☎ 702/262-5279 🕐 Thu–Sat 10.30pm–4am 🚌 Deuce 💵 Expensive

### MANDALAY BAY EVENTS CENTER
mandalaybay.com
This major venue seats 12,000 and hosts concerts and major sporting events. On some summer weekends, Mandalay Bay puts on big-names at its artificial beach.
🚩 D11 ✉ Mandalay Bay, 3950 Las Vegas Boulevard South ☎ 702/632-7777 🕐 Days and show times vary 🚌 Deuce, 203 💵 Very expensive

### MARQUEE
marqueelasvegas.com
This vast entertainment venue is perfect for 24/7 clubbers. You can

groove till late in the nightclub's three-story, LED-lit space, or bask in the sun in one of the day club's intimate infinity pools.
🚩 D9 ✉ The Cosmopolitan of Las Vegas, 3708 Las Vegas Boulevard South ☎ 702/333-9000 🕐 Fri–Sat, Mon 10pm–5am 🚌 Deuce 💵 Expensive

### MGM GRAND GARDEN ARENA
mgmgrand.com
This is one of the biggest venues in town, hosting huge events—from top entertainers to world championship boxing. It seats 16,800 and tickets can be bought several months in advance.
🚩 D10 ✉ MGM Grand, 3799 Las Vegas Boulevard South ☎ 702/891-1111 🕐 Days and showtimes vary 🚌 Deuce 💵 Expensive–very expensive

### MICHAEL JACKSON ONE
cirquedusoleil.com
The King of Pop gets Cirque du Soleil's treatment in this tribute to the musical genius, with a dramatic sequence of powerful, passionate and moving musical tableaux.
🚩 D11 ✉ Mandalay Bay, 3950 Las Vegas Boulevard South ☎ 702/632-7580 🕐 Fri–Tue 7pm and 9.30pm 🚌 Deuce, SDX 💵 Very expensive

### NAPOLEON'S LOUNGE
caesars.com/paris-las-vegas
The French theme at this cocktail lounge incorporates more than

100 varieties of champagne and European-style appetizers. Note that if you sit near the dueling pianists you may become part of their comic routine.

🔲 D9 ✉ Paris Las Vegas, 3655 Las Vegas Boulevard South ☎ 702/946-7000 🕐 Daily 6pm–2am 🚌 Deuce 💰 No cover charge

### NATHAN BURTON COMEDY MAGIC

nathanburton.com

A winner of *America's Got Talent*, Nathan Burton is an escapologist extraordinaire, whose rapid-fire tricks include the wacky and slightly risqué, as well as artful improvisation. Expect plenty of dry ice, scantily clad showgirls and hilariously set-up audience members.

✉ D9 ✉ Saxe Theater, Miracle Mile Shops, 3663 Las Vegas Boulevard South ☎ 866/932-1818 🕐 Tue–Sun 4pm 🚌 Bally's/Paris Las Vegas 🚌 Deuce 💰 Very expensive

*Penn and Teller at the Rio*

### OMNIA

omnianightclub.com

This sumptuously sexy nightclub, inside Caesars Palace's casino, has three levels and an outdoor terrace, with great views over The Strip. Each room has its own DJ playing top electro and dance music.

🔲 C8–D8 ✉ Caesars Palace, 3570 Las Vegas Boulevard South ☎ 702/785-6200 🕐 Tue, Thu–Sun 10.30pm–4am 🚇 Flamingo/Caesars Palace 🚌 Deuce 💰 Expensive

### ORLEANS ARENA

orleansarena.com

This huge arena stages top concerts and a variety of sporting events, including NCAA basketball tournaments and motocross races. It has also hosted Disney on Ice.

🔲 A10 ✉ Orleans, 4500 West Tropicana ☎ 800/745-3000 🕐 Days and showtimes vary 🚌 201 💰 Expensive–very expensive

### PARASOL DOWN

wynnlasvegas.com

Sashay down the winding staircase from the glam casino floor to this whimsically designed cocktail lounge, where colorful parasols hang overhead. Tables have straight-ahead views of the resort's glassy Lake of Dreams, with its 40ft-high (12m) waterfall.

🔲 D7–E7 ✉ Wynn Las Vegas, 3131 Las Vegas Boulevard South ☎ 702/770-7000 🕐 Daily 11am–2am 🚌 Deuce, SDX 💰 No cover charge

### THE PARK

theparkvegas.com

The Strip's newest outdoor entertainment, nightlife and dining complex revolves around the colorfully lit 40ft-high (12m) Bliss

Dance sculpture. Major sporting events and concerts are held at T-Mobile Arena and Park Theater, where you can see stars such as Bruno Mars perform.

🚇 D10 ✉ 3782 Las Vegas Boulevard South ☎ 702/693-7275 🕐 Daily (show-times vary) 🚍 Deuce 🎟 Admission free. Events: free–very expensive

## PENN & TELLER

riolasvegas.com

This talented, eccentric partnership combines magic, illusions, juggling, comedy and stunts in an intelligent show. The pair have been together for more than 30 years: Penn is big, loud and talkative, while Teller is whimsically mute. Both stay on to meet fans after every show.

🚇 B8 ✉ Rio, 3700 West Flamingo Road ☎ 702/777-2782 🕐 Sat–Wed 9pm 🚍 202 🎟 Very expensive

## PEPPERMILL FIRESIDE LOUNGE

peppermilllasvegas.com

Ankle-deep shag carpeting, fire pits, enormous white silk flowers and gushing indoor fountains are still the rage at this tribute to vintage Vegas.

🚇 E7 ✉ 2985 Las Vegas Boulevard South ☎ 702/735-4177 🕐 Daily 24 hours 🚍 Deuce, SDX 🎟 No cover charge

## ROYAL LINKS GOLF CLUB

royallinksgolfclub.com

This course has holes based on those from famous British Open courses, including St. Andrews, Royal Troon, Carnoustie and Turnberry. The 18th hole looks like a medieval castle.

🚇 Off map ✉ 5995 East Vegas Valley Drive, 8 miles (13km) east of The Strip ☎ 702/765-0484 🕐 Daily (opening hours vary) 🚍 SX 🎟 Very expensive

## SKYFALL LOUNGE

delanolasvegas

Mix good music, savvy DJs, great cocktails, an innovative bar menu, tasty tapas and views from 64 floors up and you have one of The Strip's most fashionable spots. Reserve a table indoors or go out on the balcony.

🚇 D11 ✉ Delano Las Vegas at Mandalay Bay, 3950 Las Vegas Boulevard South ☎ 702/632-7575 🕐 Sun–Thu 5pm–midnight, Fri–Sat 5pm–1.30am 🚍 Deuce, SDX 🎟 Usually no cover charge

## THOMAS & MACK CENTER

thomasandmack.com

This state-of-the-art, multipurpose arena, seating 19,500, stages world-class entertainment and major national sports events. These range from monster-truck racing, boxing and rodeos to concerts, basketball and ice shows.

🚇 G10 ✉ University of Nevada, Las Vegas (UNLV), 4505 South Maryland Parkway ☎ 702/739-32671 🕐 Days and showtimes vary 🚍 108 🎟 Expensive–very expensive

## UNLV ARTS CENTER

pac.unlv.edu

See major international artists perform classical and popular music, dance, theater, ballet and opera. The center comprises the Artemus W. Ham Concert Hall, home to symphony orchestra and chamber music recitals, and the Judy Bayley Theatre.

➕ G9 ✉ University of Nevada, Las Vegas (UNLV), 4505 South Maryland Parkway ☎ 702/895-3535 🕐 Days and showtimes vary 🚍 109 💵 Expensive–very expensive

### V THEATER
vtheaterboxoffice.com
This specially tailored venue, next door to Planet Hollywood, showcases a varied program during the day and evening, from comedy, variety and magic to game shows and tribute acts.

➕ D9 ✉ Miracle Mile Shops, 3663 Las Vegas Boulevard South ☎ 702/260-7200 🕐 Daily (show times vary) 🚍 Deuce 💵 Expensive–very expensive

### VEGAS INDOOR SKYDIVING
vegasindoorskydiving.com
Test your skills at this exciting new sporting challenge. A vertical wind tunnel simulates an authentic free-fall experience of skydiving in a column of air, with vertical airspeeds of up to 120mph (193kph). No experience is needed though there are some maximum weight limits and other restrictions.

➕ E7 ✉ 200 Convention Center Drive ☎ 702/731-4768 🕐 Daily 9.45–8 🚍 108, Deuce, SDX 💵 Expensive

### WESTGATE LAS VEGAS RESORT & CASINO
westgatedestinations.com
A variety of talented musicians, comedians and magicians perform here. Formerly the Las Vegas Hilton, where Elvis staged a comeback in 1976, it stages big acts at the International Westgate Theater and smaller comedy and magic, showgirl revues and live music in the Westgate Cabaret.

➕ F7 ✉ 3000 Paradise Road ☎ 702/732-5111 🕐 Days and showtimes vary 🚍 Las Vegas Convention Center 🚍 108 💵 Expensive–very expensive

### XS
xslasvegas.com
After dark on The Strip, you'll find the most fashionable crowd in Las Vegas poolside at the Encore Beach Club. On some hot, sultry Sunday evenings during summer, come for "nightswim" pool parties. Dress to impress, no jeans.

➕ E7 ✉ Encore at Wynn Las Vegas, 3131 Las Vegas Boulevard South ☎ 702/770-0097 🕐 Fri–Mon 10pm–4am 🚍 Deuce, SDX 💵 Expensive

*Simulated skydiving in a wind tunnel*

# Eat

There are places to eat across the city to suit all tastes and budgets. In this section establishments are listed alphabetically.

# Introduction

In the last decade, the dining scene in Las Vegas has heated up, especially with the arrival of world-famous chefs and celebrity restaurant owners on The Strip.

### So What's on Offer?

The famous Vegas buffet has become much more exciting and provides something for everyone at a reasonable price. There are endless top-class establishments where you can feast on the superb cuisine of Michelin-star chefs, and there's also the opportunity to dine at a restaurant run by a celebrity chef. The sheer variety of cuisine is astonishing, from fine French, Italian and Chinese to Mediterranean, Thai/Korean fusion and Pacific Rim. All-night casino coffee shops still play an important role, as do traditional steak houses.

### Dining Tips

It can be hard to get a table at high-end restaurants, especially on Friday and Saturday nights. Plan ahead—you can reserve up to 30 days or more in advance. Many of these open for dinner only. Mid-range eateries are more likely to be open all day, and you will likely not need a reservation for breakfast or lunch. Most major hotels have a fast-food court to grab a quick bite, and many have a buffet open for breakfast, lunch and dinner. Buffet lines can be long, so allow plenty of time.

---

### DINNER SHOWS

Take advantage of one of the dinner shows on offer, where you can eat and be thoroughly entertained at the same time. Probably the most popular of these for families is the Tournament of Kings at the Excalibur (▷ 68), where your meal is accompanied by a jousting tournament, dragons, wizards and great special effects. Many other casinos on the Strip offer special pre-show dinner menus, including at restaurants at Bellagio, Caesars Palace, MGM Grand and Wynn Las Vegas.

---

*From top: all types of food are on offer around the clock; the Lago Bar at the Bellagio; a café on the replica of St. Mark's Square; Joël Robuchon's restaurant*

# Directory

## South Strip

**Buffets**
Bayside Buffet
**Cafés, Pubs and Lounges**
Il Fornaio Panetteria & Restaurant
Veranda Bar
**European**
Jaleo
Joël Robuchon
Red Square
**International**
Fleur
RX Boiler Room
**Mexican**
Border Grill
Tacos & Tequila (T&T)
**Modern American**
Aureole
**Steaks and Seafood**
Charlie Palmer Steak
Craftsteak
Emeril's New Orleans Fish House

## Center Strip

**Asian/Fusion**
China Poblano
Koi
Momofuku
Nobu
**Buffets**
Bacchanal Buffet
The Buffet
Carnival World & Seafood Buffet
Wicked Spoon
**Cafés, Pubs & Lounges**
Gordon Ramsay Pub & Grill
Hash House a Go Go
Holsteins Shakes and Buns
Jean Philippe Patisserie
Yardbird Southern Table & Bar
**French**
Bouchon
Mon Ami Gabi
Picasso
**Italian**
Battista's Hole in the Wall

Canaletto
GIADA
Lago
OTTO Enoteca Pizzeria
Rao's
**Mexican/Southwestern**
China Poblano
Mesa Grill
**Steaks and Seafood**
Lawry's The Prime Rib
Michael Mina
Pampas Brazilian Grille
Strip House

## North Strip

**Asian/Fusion**
Andrea's
Lotus of Siam
RA Sushi
**European**
Top of the World
**Italian**
Piero's
**North American and Mexican**
Johnny Rocket's
**Steaks and Seafood**
ENVY
THE Steak House

## Downtown

**Asian/Fusion**
Lillie's Asian Cuisine
Second Street Grill
**Buffets**
Garden Court Buffet
**Cafés, Pubs & Lounges**
Binion's Café
**European**
Hugo's Cellar
**Mexican**
Doña Maria Tamales
**Steaks and Seafood**
Top of Binion's Steakhouse
Triple George Grill

EAT

# Eating A–Z

| PRICES | |
|---|---|
| Prices are approximate, based on a 3-course meal for one person. | |
| $$$ | over $50 |
| $$ | $20–$50 |
| $ | under $20 |

## ANDREA'S $$$

wynnlasvegas.com

Act cool when you see celebrities dining here. Down-tempo DJ beats whirl around leather sofas, while servers drop off Asian-influenced dishes like five-spice lobster and steaks with wasabi demi-glace sauce at the low-slung tables.

🔢 D7–E7 ✉ Encore at Wynn Las Vegas, 3131 Las Vegas Boulevard South ☎ 702/770-5340 🕐 Sun–Thu 6–10.30pm, Fri–Sat 6–11.30pm 🚌 Deuce, SDX

## AUREOLE $$$

charliepalmer.com/aureole-las-vegas/

Renowned chef Charlie Palmer's restaurant has big windows, glass-covered views of waterfalls and a massive award-winning wine tower, holding 3,200-plus bottles. American meat and seafood dishes dominate the first-class, seasonally changing menu here.

🔢 D11 ✉ Mandalay Bay, 3950 Las Vegas Boulevard South ☎ 702/632-7401 🕐 Mon–Sat 5.30–10.30pm 🚌 Deuce, SDX

## BACCHANAL BUFFET $$

caesars.com/caesars-palace

The Strip's most expensive casino buffet is the reigning champion when it comes to satisfying all-you-can-eat feasts with more than 500 dishes. The huge refurbished dining space looks out onto the Garden of the Gods.

🔢 C8–D8 ✉ Caesars Palace, 3570 Las Vegas Boulevard South ☎ 702/732-7928 🕐 Mon–Fri 7.30am–10pm, Sat–Sun 8am–10pm 🚇 Flamingo/Caesars Palace 🚌 Deuce

## BATTISTA'S HOLE IN THE WALL $$

battistaslasvegas.com

For more than 45 years tourists and locals alike have been flocking here for the excellent Italian-American comfort food, served with heart-warming style.

🔢 D9 ✉ 4041 LINQ Lane ☎ 702/732-1424 🕐 Daily 5–10.30pm 🚇 Flamingo/Caesars Palace 🚌 Deuce, SDX

## BAYSIDE BUFFET $$

mandalaybay.com

Floor-to-ceiling windows give sweeping views of the tropical lagoon outside. Although the buffet is not over-large, the cuisine is very good, with excellent salads, hearty meats and one of The Strip's better dessert selections, all made on the premises.

🔢 D11 ✉ Mandalay Bay, 3950 Las Vegas Boulevard South ☎ 702/632-7402 🕐 Daily 7–2.30, 4.45–9.45 🚌 Deuce, SDX

## BINION'S CAFÉ $

binions.com

If you're looking for a great place for a light snack or something more substantial at a low price, try this simple no-frills café. The breakfasts are particularly good.

🔢 G3 ✉ Binion's, 128 Fremont Street ☎ 702/382-1600 🕐 Daily 7am–2am 🚌 Deuce, SDX

## BORDER GRILL $$

bordergrill.com

Come here for great Mexican cooking and California-influenced fusion tastes in a lively, colorful setting. Lunch on TV chefs Susan Feniger and Mary Sue Milliken's spicy baby chilaquiles and chicken tamales on the patio or get a take-out taco.

🔢 D11 ✉ Mandalay Bay, 3950 Las Vegas Boulevard South ☎ 702/632-7403 🕐 Mon–Fri 11–10, Sat 10am–11pm, Sun 10–10 🚌 Deuce, SDX

## BOUCHON $$

thomaskeller.com/bouchonlasvegas
World-renowned chef Thomas Keller showcases his French bistro fare at Bouchon, located in the Venezia Tower. Dark wooden seating, antique lights, a mosaic tile floor and hand-painted murals provide a café-style ambience amid a poolside garden.

🔢 D8 ✉ The Venetian, 3355 Las Vegas Boulevard South ☎ 702/414-6200 🕐 Mon–Fri 7am–1pm, Sat–Sun 7am–2pm, daily 5–10pm 🚌 Deuce

## THE BUFFET $$

This is one of the most highly regarded, albeit most expensive, buffets on The Strip. It offers many different types of cuisine, including Italian and Asian in a European marketplace-style setting.

🔢 C9–D9 ✉ Bellagio, 3600 Las Vegas Boulevard South ☎ 702/693-7111 🕐 Daily 7am–10pm 🚌 Deuce, SDX

## CANALETTO $$

ilfornaio.com/canalettolasvegas
Where better to sample northern Italian cuisine than on a re-creation of Venice's St. Mark's Square? Some little-known Italian wines are on offer to complement choices such as wood-fired pizza, saffron risotto or tagliatelle pasta with brandy cream sauce.

🔢 D8 ✉ Grand Canal Shoppes, 3377 Las Vegas Boulevard South ☎ 702/733-0070 🕐 Sun–Thu 11.30–11, Fri–Sat 11.30–midnight 🚌 Deuce

## CARNIVAL WORLD & SEAFOOD BUFFET $$

caesars.com/rio-las-vegas
This is one of the best buffets in Las Vegas, with chefs cooking on view at various points around the serving islands. There are almost a dozen styles of cuisine on offer, from Italian gelato to Asian barbecue. Fresh seafood is the house specialty.

🔢 B8 ✉ Rio All-Suite Hotel & Casino, 3700 West Flamingo Road ☎ 702/777-7757 🕐 Daily 8am–10pm 🚌 202

## CHARLIE PALMER STEAK $$$

charliepalmer.com
Gleaming woodwork and leather banquettes set the scene for a meal that might include charcoal-grilled filet mignon, a porterhouse steak for two with truffled potato gratin or steamed halibut.

🔢 D11 ✉ Four Seasons Las Vegas, 3960 Las Vegas Boulevard South ☎ 702/632-5120 🕐 Mon–Sat 5–10.30pm 🚌 Deuce, SDX

## CHINA POBLANO $$

chinapoblano.com
East meets West here, with a menu offering some of the best-known dishes from Mexico and China—separate, not fusion—in a colorful, smart setting. Choose from tacos, dim sum, noodles, ceviche and more. The cocktails are imaginative.

🔢 D9 ✉ The Cosmopolitan of Las Vegas, 3708 Las Vegas Boulevard South ☎ 702/698-7900 🕐 Sun–Thu 11.30–11, Fri–Sat 11.30–11.30 🚌 Deuce

## CHILD-FRIENDLY

Apart from the usual fast-food chains, Las Vegas has many more options to keep your kids happy. Buffets enable them to pick and choose what they like, and most have an ice cream machine. Theme restaurants are increasingly rare on The Strip these days, but the whole family can sing along with the 1950s-styled servers at Roxy's Diner at the Stratosphere (✉ 2000 Las Vegas Boulevard South ☎ 702/380-7777 ⏰ Daily 24 hours).

## CRAFTSTEAK $$$

craftsteaklasvegas.com
Hand-selected beef from small farms and artisan producers is served here, with the magic touch of award-winning chef Tom Colicchio. The vegetable sides are not an afterthought here: sample garlicky heirloom cauliflower or butternut squash with nut streusel.
➕ D10 ✉ MGM Grand, 3799 Las Vegas Boulevard South ☎ 702/891-7318 ⏰ Sun–Thu 5–10pm, Fri–Sat 5–10.30pm 🚇 MGM Grand 🚌 Deuce, SDX

## DOÑA MARIA TAMALES $

donamariatamales.com
The tamales at this Mexican restaurant are great. Choose from shredded chicken in spicy green sauce, Monterey Jack cheese with green chilies or pork in red sauce, all wrapped in cornmeal.
➕ G4 ✉ 910 Las Vegas Boulevard South ☎ 702/382-6538 ⏰ Daily 8am–10pm 🚌 Deuce, SDX

## EMERIL'S NEW ORLEANS FISH HOUSE $$$

mgmgrand.com
This is a scaled-down re-creation of Emeril Lagasse's New Orleans restaurant, specializing in spicy Creole/Cajun recipes. The menu includes barbecued shrimp, jumbo crab cakes, fried frog legs, Louisiana-style broiled oysters and sumptuous banana cream pie drizzled with caramel.
➕ D10 ✉ MGM Grand, 3799 Las Vegas Boulevard South ☎ 702/891-7374 ⏰ Daily 11.30–10 🚌 Deuce, SDX

## ENVY $$$

renaissancelasvegas.com
In this svelte dining room near the convention center, top-quality fresh ingredients appear in innovative dishes, redefining the usual steak-house offerings. Soothing red shades give a sophisticated feel. It's also popular for power breakfasts.
➕ F7 ✉ Renaissance, 3400 Paradise Road ☎ 702/784-5716 ⏰ Daily 6.30–11, 5–10 🚇 Las Vegas Convention Center 🚌 108

## FLEUR $$$

hubertkeller.com
Celebrity chef Hubert Keller serves bold, international fusion cuisine. Nibble on Parmesan paprika popcorn or blow your budget on the $5,000 FleurBurger: wagyu minced beef, foie gras and truffles, washed down with 1995 Chateau Petrus. The small tapas-style dishes are ideal for sharing.
➕ D11 ✉ Mandalay Bay, 3950 Las Vegas Boulevard South ☎ 702/632-7200 ⏰ Sun–Thu 11–10, Fri–Sat 11–10.30 🚌 Deuce, SDX

## GARDEN COURT BUFFET $

mainstreetcasino.com
Watch your food being prepared for you at what is said to be Downtown's best buffet. Choices include Mexican, Asian and American, and there are specialty

nights such as seafood dinners on Friday or prime rib and scampi on Saturday evenings.

➕ G2 ✉ Main Street Station, 200 North Main Street ☎ 702/387-1896 🕐 Sun–Thu 7am–9pm, Fri–Sat 7am–10pm 🚌 Deuce, SDX

## GIADA $$$

giadadelaurentiis.com/vegas

TV celebrity chef Giada de Laurentiis personally oversees the menu at this light-filled dining room hung with vintage Italian cinema posters. House-made Italian antipasti and salumi are always good bets, as is the lemon-pesto grilled cheese sandwich at weekend brunch.

➕ D9 ✉ The Cromwell, 3595 Las Vegas Boulevard South ☎ 855/442-3271 🕐 Daily 8am–11pm 🚉 Flamingo/Caesars Palace 🚌 Deuce

## GORDON RAMSAY PUB & GRILL $$

The notoriously no-nonsense British chef introduces Vegas to the culinary delights of the British pub, with two connected restaurants offering traditional dishes, including fish and chips and shepherd's pie, plus a wide choice of beers.

➕ C8–D8 ✉ Caesars Palace, 3570 Las Vegas Boulevard South ☎ 702/731-7410 🕐 Sun–Thu 11–11, Fri–Sat 11–midnight 🚉 Flamingo/Caesars Palace 🚌 Deuce

## HASH HOUSE A GO GO $$

hashhouseagogo.com/vegas

Plates of farm food with a twist are so huge that most people feel full for the entire day afterward. Sage fried chicken over waffles, corned beef hash and bloody Marys are all brunch favorites.

➕ D8–D9 ✉ The LINQ Hotel & Casino, 3535 Las Vegas Boulevard South ☎ 702/254-4646 🕐 Daily 24 hours 🚉 Harrah's/The LINQ 🚌 Deuce

## HOLSTEINS SHAKES AND BUNS $$

holsteinsburgers.com/lasvegas

One of The Strip's most popular burger bars, Holsteins dishes up towering stacks of fried onion rings and deluxe burgers. Pair your burger with "bamboozled" milk-shakes spiked with liqueurs, flavored vodkas and nostalgic candy, or go for an American craft beer.

➕ D9 ✉ The Cosmopolitan of Las Vegas, 3708 Las Vegas Boulevard South ☎ 702/698-7940 🕐 Mon–Thu 11am–midnight, Fri–Sat 11am–2am, Sun 10am–midnight 🚌 Deuce

## HUGO'S CELLAR $$$

hugoscellar.com

Below street level, this romantic restaurant has a touch of old-school class. Each woman receives a red rose as she enters the low-lit, dark-wood space. There's excellent Continental cuisine and some dishes are prepared at the table.

➕ G3 ✉ Four Queens, 202 Fremont Street ☎ 702/385-4011 🕐 Daily 5–10pm 🚌 Deuce, SDX

### BUFFET KNOW-HOW

Buffets offer breakfast, lunch and dinner. They are a great option for families because there is sure to be something for everyone. Buffets also offer value for money. This does, of course, mean that they are popular and lines can be long, especially at peak times. At the most popular buffets, you may need to allow up to two to three hours for your meal.

EAT

## IL FORNAIO PANETTERIA & RESTAURANT $–$$

ilfornaio.com/lasvegas

It's worth making a special trip to this Italian bakery café just for its espresso-mocha scones with chocolate chunks. Italian-American breakfasts, lunches and dinners are served in the restaurant.

🔢 D10 ✉ New York-New York, 3790 Las Vegas Boulevard South ☎ 702/650-6500 🕐 Panetteria: daily 6am–5.30pm. Restaurant: daily 7.30–10.30am, Sun–Thu 11.30–11, Fri–Sat 11.30am–midnight 🚌 MGM Grand 🚍 Deuce, SDX

## JALEO $$

jaleo.com

Celebrity master chef José Andrés brings the best of Spanish cuisine to Vegas. Besides the delectable tapas snacks, try Jaleo's Ibérico-cured Spanish ham, or its classic paella, cooked over a wood fire.

🔢 D9 ✉ The Cosmopolitan of Las Vegas, 3708 Las Vegas Boulevard South ☎ 702/698-7950 🕐 Sun–Thu noon–11pm, Fr–Sat noon–midnight 🚍 Deuce

## JEAN PHILIPPE PATISSERIE $

arialasvegas.com

This chic little café serves cakes and pastries that are almost too pretty to eat, and possibly the best *croque-monsieur* in town. Its adjacent shop sells gourmet chocolates. The original location at the Bellagio has the world's largest chocolate fountain on display.

🔢 C10 ✉ Aria, 3730 Las Vegas Boulevard South ☎ 702/590-8550 🕐 Mon–Thu 6am–midnight, Fri–Sun till 1am 🚍 Deuce

## JOËL ROBUCHON $$$

mgmgrand.com

Robuchon's reputation for the highest standards is upheld here. The sophisticated 16-course fine French menu is an experience, or if you prefer a scaled-down version, choose the four-course tasting menu.

🔢 D10 ✉ MGM Grand, 3799 Las Vegas Boulevard South ☎ 702/891-7925 🕐 Daily 5.30–10pm 🚌 MGM Grand 🚍 Deuce, SDX

## JOHNNY ROCKETS $

johnnyrockets.com

The servers at this American retro diner, which serves burgers, tasty fries, club sandwiches, great malts and shakes, wear outfits straight out of a 1950s soda fountain. It's kid-friendly and conveniently located for shopaholic families.

🔢 D7 ✉ Fashion Show, 3200 Las Vegas Boulevard South ☎ 702/784-0107 🕐 Mon–Sat 9–9, Sun 11–7 🚍 Deuce, SDX

## KOI $$$

koirestaurant.com

This outpost of the New York City hotspot exudes a sophisticated

---

### EATING ON A BUDGET

If you are on a budget you have several options for eating inexpensively. So long as you keep playing, most casinos will ply you with free food and drink—though take care not to spend more than you save. There are plenty of well-known fast food chains on The Strip, if all you want is to refuel on the go. Try the various food courts inside casinos and shopping malls on The Strip and beyond, such as Las Vegas Chinatown Plaza (▷ 119). Many informal restaurants, such as the Peppermill, at 2985 Las Vegas Boulevard South, serve large portions, and are happy to provide take-out containers for leftovers.

tone. Koi cooks up modern and traditional Japanese-inspired dishes with a Californian accent; try the Kobe beef carpaccio with fried shiitake mushrooms and yuzu vinaigrette, with the best views of Bellagio's fountains.

🚩 D9 ✉ Planet Hollywood, 3667 Las Vegas Boulevard South ☎ 702/454-4555 ⏰ Sun–Thu 5.30–10.30pm, Fri–Sat 5.30–11.30pm 🚍 Deuce

## LAGO $$

bellagio.com/lago
From talented chef Julian Serrano, this sleek lakeside dining room at Bellagio offers modern Italian cuisine with an artistic touch. Come for three-course tasting menus at lunch or Sunday brunches with house-made pastry baskets and tiramisu for dessert.

🚩 C9–D9 ✉ Bellagio, 3600 Las Vegas Boulevard South ☎ 702/693-8865 ⏰ Mon–Thu 11.30am–11pm, Fri–Sat 11.30am–midnight, Sun 10.30am–11pm 🚍 Deuce, SDX

## LAWRY'S THE PRIME RIB $$$

lawrysonline.com
Lawry's is popular for its perfectly cooked, tasty prime rib. Servers in stylish uniforms and starched white caps tend to your every need in the art deco surroundings.

🚩 E9 ✉ 4043 Howard Hughes Parkway ☎ 702/893-2223 ⏰ Mon–Fri 11.30–2, Sat–Thu 5–10pm, Sun 4–9pm 🚍 202

## LILLIE'S ASIAN CUISINE $$

goldennugget.com
There's an ecletic mix of cuisines here, but the menu is mostly Chinese with good quality Sichuan and Cantonese dishes, plus Japanese dishes served on hibachi hot griddles.

Mon Ami

🚩 G3 ✉ Golden Nugget, 129 Fremont Street ☎ 702/386-8131 ⏰ Daily 5pm–midnight 🚍 Deuce, SDX

## LOTUS OF SIAM $

lotusofsiamlv.com
Lotus of Siam is one of the top Thai restaurants in Las Vegas, with a huge menu of dishes. Let them know how hot you like your food, and if you overdo it, order the coconut ice cream for dessert.

🚩 G6 ✉ 953 East Sahara Avenue ☎ 702/735-3033 ⏰ Mon–Fri 11.30–2.30, daily 5.30–10pm 🚍 SDX

## MESA GRILL $$$

mesagrill.com
Sample modern US Southwestern-Mexican fusion cuisine from celebrity chef Bobby Flay, whose specialties include ancho chile and honey-glazed salmon and blue corn lobster tacos. The fruit margaritas will leave you glowing.

🚩 C8–D8 ✉ Caesars Palace, 3570 Las Vegas Boulevard South ☎ 877/346-4642 ⏰ Mon–Fri 11–2.30, 5–11, Sat–Sun 10.30–3, 5–11 🚇 Flamingo/Caesars Palace 🚍 Deuce

## MICHAEL MINA $$$

michaelmina.net

Enjoy seafood favorites that chef Michael Mina has made famous with his daring approach, using unexpected flavors and textures blended with Mediterranean and Californian ingredients. Sleek, yet casual, this is the perfect place to try Mina's signature dishes.

🔲 C9–D9 ⊠ Bellagio, 3600 Las Vegas Boulevard South ☎ 702/693-8865 🕙 Mon–Sat 5.30–10pm 🚌 Deuce, SDX

## MOMOFUKU $$$

vegas.momofuku.com

Renegade New York City chef David Chang has brought his game-changing cuisine to The Strip. Feast on dishes showing American, Korean and Japanese influences, such as black truffle ramen, roasted beets with XO sauce or puffy shrimp buns with spicy mayo.

🔲 D9 ⊠ The Cosmopolitan of Las Vegas, 3708 Las Vegas Boulevard South ☎ 702/698-2663 🕙 Daily 11.30am–2pm, 5–11pm 🚌 Deuce

## MON AMI GABI $$

monamigabi.com

Fine French fare is served in the sunlit atrium or on the patio under the faux Eiffel Tower. Tables are set beneath sparkling lights, with a great view of the Bellagio's famous fountain show.

🔲 D9 ⊠ Paris Las Vegas, 3655 Las Vegas Boulevard South ☎ 702/944-4224 🕙 Sun–Thu 7am–11pm, Fri–Sat 7am–midnight 🚆 Bally's/Paris 🚌 Deuce, SDX

## NOBU $$$

noburestaurants.com

This is the largest branch of one of the most popular Japanese-fusion restaurants in the US. Specialties include black cod with miso, or try the blow-out multi-course *omakase*-tasting menu, created daily in chef Matsuhisa's signature culinary style.

🔲 C8–D8 ⊠ Caesars Palace, 3570 Las Vegas Boulevard South ☎ 702/785-6674 🕙 Sun–Thu 5–11pm, Fri–Sat 5pm–midnight 🚆 Flamingo/Caesars Palace 🚌 Deuce

## OTTO ENOTECA PIZZERIA $$

lasvegas.ottopizzeria.com

Savor celebrity chef Mario Batali's authentic Italian dishes with a bottle from Joe Bastianich's curated wine list in the elegant dining room or in the more casual café looking out on bustling St. Mark's Square.

🔲 D8 ⊠ The Venetian, 3355 Las Vegas Boulevard South ☎ 702/677-3390 🕙 Daily 11–11 🚌 Deuce

## PAMPAS BRAZILIAN GRILLE $$$

pampasusa.com

Come here to enjoy an authentic taste of Brazil. Helpful servers bring the sizzling skewers of the finest meats to your table in an endless parade while you feast on mountains of fresh salads, soups, vegetables and desserts at the appetizing buffet.

---

### DINING WITH A VIEW

There are some wonderful spots in Vegas where you can savor great views while you eat, but one of the best is the Top of the World restaurant (▷ 149). On the 106th floor of the Stratosphere Tower, it makes one revolution in 60 minutes, during which you can see The Strip, the mountains, the valleys and beyond. Also try Mon Ami Gabi (▷ 145).

---

**EAT**

D9 ✉ Miracle Mile Shops, 3663 Las Vegas Boulevard South ☎ 702/737-4748 🕓 Sun–Thu 11.30am–10.30pm, Fri–Sat 11.30am–11.30pm 🚌 Deuce

### PICASSO $$$

bellagiolasvegas.com

This is among the most highly rated restaurants in Vegas. The refined cuisine reflects places in which the artist lived (south of France and Spain), and there are more than 1,500 bottles of the finest European wine. The Picassos on the walls are authentic.

➕ C9–D9 ✉ Bellagio, 3600 Las Vegas Boulevard South ☎ 702/693-8865 🕓 Wed–Mon 5.30–9.30pm 🚌 Deuce, SDX

### PIERO'S $$$

pieroscuisine.com

Sublime Italian cuisine is served at Piero's, one of the city's oldest established restaurants. Former patrons include Michael Jordan, Arnold Schwarzenegger and Keith Richards. Osso bucco, one of Piero's signature dishes, melts in the mouth, and the fish and sea-food are also excellent.

➕ E7 ✉ 335 Convention Center Drive ☎ 702/369-2305 🕓 Daily 5.30–10pm 🚌 108

### RA SUSHI $$

rasushi.com

An upbeat, casual mood creates the perfect setting to enjoy fresh sushi, Japanese-fusion cuisine and signature dishes so good that you can't wait to return. Bright wall hangings and globe lighting accent the interior.

➕ D7–D8 ✉ Fashion Show, 3200 Las Vegas Boulevard South ☎ 702/696-0008 🕓 Sun–Thu 11am–midnight, Fri–Sat 11am–1am 🚌 Deuce, SDX

---

**JUST DESSERTS**

If you're after dessert then head to Jean Philippe Patisserie at Aria (▷ 144) or the Bellagio (▷ 14–15) for pastries, eclairs and cookies. At The Venetian (▷ 58–59), Bouchon Bakery also has pastries and cookies, as does Payard Patisserie inside Caesars Palace (▷ 16–17).

---

### RAO'S $$$

raosrestaurants.com

This highly rated family-run Italian restaurant from New York City serves traditional dishes, using the best ingredients. Try the giant house-made meatballs in marinara sauce, the osso bucco or Uncle Vincent's succulent lemon chicken.

➕ C8–D8 ✉ Caesars Palace, 3570 Las Vegas Boulevard South ☎ 702/731-7267 🕓 Sun–Thu 5–10pm, Fri–Sat 5–10.30pm 🚝 Flamingo/Caesars Palace 🚌 Deuce

### RED SQUARE $$$

mandalaybay.com

Wash latkes and blinis down with vodka at the ice-topped bar, or choose US and Italian dishes in this Russian-theme restaurant, where the headless statue of Lenin, the red-velvet drapes and the fake communist propaganda give the game away.

➕ D11 ✉ Mandalay Bay, 3950 Las Vegas Boulevard South ☎ 702/632-7200 🕓 Sun–Thu 4–10pm, Fri–Sat 4–11pm 🚝 Flamingo/Caesars Palace 🚌 Deuce, SDX

### RX BOILER ROOM $$

rxboilerroom.com

From tacos to lobster to 18-hour Guinness-braised short ribs, chef Rick Moonen immerses guests in a shared dining experience.

**EAT**

➕ D11 ✉ Mandalay Bay, 3950 Las Vegas Boulevard South ☎ 702/632-7200 🕐 Daily 5–11pm 🚌 Deuce, SDX

## SECOND STREET GRILL $$

fremontcasino.com

Step back in time at this hidden gem and sample good Pacific Rim and contemporary cuisine at affordable prices. Soft lighting and rich woods encourage you to relax in the oversized banquettes.

➕ G3 ✉ Fremont Casino, 200 Fremont Street ☎ 702/385-3232 🕐 Sun–Mon, Thu 5–10pm, Fri–Sat 5–11pm 🚌 Deuce, SDX

## THE STEAK HOUSE $$$

circuscircus.com

This old-timer is popular for its prime ribs and mesquite charcoal-grilled steaks at reasonable prices. Seafood, lobster, chicken and lamb are also on the menu, all accompanied by side dishes like baked potatoes and green salads.

➕ E6 ✉ Circus Circus, 2880 Las Vegas Boulevard South ☎ 702/794-3767 🕐 Sun–Fri 4–10pm, Sat 4–11pm 🚌 Deuce

## STRIP HOUSE $$$

striphouse.com

Excellent American cuisine is served in this intimate restaurant, whose walls are lined with retro black-and-white portraits of magazine pin-up models. The steaks are for serious carnivores, going up to the massive 20 oz (565g) New York Strip. There's also an impressive rare scotch menu to work your way through.

➕ D9 ✉ Planet Hollywood, 3667 Las Vegas Boulevard South ☎ 702/737-5200 🕐 Sun–Thu 5–11pm, Fri–Sat 5–11.30pm 🚌 Deuce

## TACOS & TEQUILA (T&T) $$

tacosandtequilalv.com

Enjoy some traditional as well as more innovative Mexican dishes and cocktails at this modernist, mural-adorned restaurant. Order a shot of tequila or a juicy margarita to go with your spicy tacos, fajitas, enchiladas and burritos.

➕ C11–D11 ✉ Luxor, 3900 Las Vegas Boulevard South ☎ 702/262-5225 🕐 Daily 11–11 🚌 Deuce

*Dining at the Stratosphere Tower's Top of the World revolving restaurant*

## TOP OF BINION'S STEAKHOUSE $$$

binions.com

Settle down to delicious succulent steaks and chops while taking in the spectacular views of Las Vegas from the 24th floor. The vibe here is vintage Vegas, with a crowd of die-hard gamblers, cowboys wearing Stetson hats and tourists.

🔳 G3 ✉ Binion's, 128 Fremont Street ☎ 702/382-1600 🕐 Daily 5–10pm 🚍 Deuce, SDX

## TOP OF THE WORLD $$$

topoftheworldlv.com

Master chefs Rick Giffen and Claude Gaty have achieved the seemingly impossible at this stylish revolving restaurant: to upstage the best view in the city. The menu gives traditional French cuisine flavor-packed Asian twists, such as crab cakes with ginger slaw, or try the tasting menu.

🔳 E5–F5 ✉ Stratosphere Tower, 2000 Las Vegas Boulevard South ☎ 702/380-7711 🕐 Daily 11–11 🚍 Deuce

## TRIPLE GEORGE GRILL $$–$$$

triplegeorgegrill.com

This sophisticated Downtown grill offers reliable steaks and chops, fine seafood dishes, fantastic desserts and serious cocktails. Portions are big so you may want to share a main course.

🔳 G3 ✉ 201 North Third Street ☎ 702/384-2761 🕐 Mon–Fri 11–10, Sat–Sun 4–10 🚍 Deuce

## VERANDA BAR $$

fourseasons.com/lasvegas

Bright and airy in the daytime, low lit and intimate after dark, this elegant but casual snack and cocktail bar offers a wide range of tasty Italian antipasti and light dishes, which are ideal for a quick bite before a show.

🔳 D11 ✉ Four Seasons, 3960 Las Vegas Boulevard South ☎ 702/632-5000 🕐 Daily 11–10 🚍 Deuce

## WICKED SPOON $$

cosmopolitanlasvegas.com

The tiny plates let hungry diners cram even more onto their trays at this elevated Vegas buffet. The dessert area offers endless choices, and more than a dozen hot-food stations have options not easily found elsewhere, such as bone marrow and paella.

🔳 D9 ✉ The Cosmopolitan of Las Vegas, 3708 Las Vegas Boulevard South ☎ 877/893-2001 🕐 Mon–Thu 8am–2pm & 5–9pm, Fri–Sat 8am–10pm, Sun 8am–9pm 🚍 Deuce

## YARDBIRD SOUTHERN TABLE & BAR $$

runchickenrun.com

Scratch an itch for good, ol' Southern favorites like buttermilk fried chicken, BBQ pork ribs, okra and fluffy biscuits at this laid-back dining lounge. Cocktails in mason jars and a long list of bourbons and craft beers are kept on hand.

🔳 D8 ✉ Grand Canal Shoppes, 3355 Las Vegas Boulevard South ☎ 702/297-6541 🕐 Mon–Fri 11–11, Sat–Sun 10am–11pm 🚍 Deuce

**EAT**

# Sleep

**With options ranging from luxurious to budget motels, Las Vegas has accommodations to suit everyone. In this section establishments are listed alphabetically.**

# Introduction

Las Vegas is one of the few cities where you can eat, drink, shop and be entertained without even needing to leave your hotel.

## Hotels

For a truly unique experience, stay in one of the theme casino hotels on and around The Strip. These are like no others in the world and give you the added benefit of being right in the heart of the action. An increasing number of smaller, more exclusive hotels are popping up that offer an alternative for those who want time out away from the neon jungle. The north end of The Strip has seen better days in places. A few bastions of the "Golden Era" remain but most have undergone extensive renovations, while others are being torn down to make way for dazzling new resorts. If you want a taste of nostalgia, choose a hotel in historic Downtown, a favorite with millions of visitors.

## Motels

Las Vegas boasts dozens of motels near The Strip and Downtown. Rates can be rock-bottom and their rooms are normally the last to get booked up, making them a good bet for finding a last-minute room. Most motels don't have casinos, which also means they are also lacking large crowds. Don't expect much more than standard motel lodgings.

### GETTING THE BEST DEAL

For the best deal start looking well in advance: In Las Vegas it really does pay to shop around. Set a budget, know where you would like to stay and in what type of accommodations. Generally, prices are lower during the week but room rates fluctuate according to demand—they can change from day to day. Check to see if the city is staging a major convention before deciding when to go, as accommodations will be in demand, making prices higher. If you do your homework first, it's possible to get a luxury hotel room at a budget price.

*From top: Circus Circus, one of the oldest hotels on The Strip; the lobby of The Palazzo; the pool at the Aria*

SLEEP

# Directory

## South Strip

**Budget**
Excalibur
Monte Carlo
**Mid-Range**
Doubletree by Hilton
Luxor
Mandalay Bay
MGM Grand
New York New York
Tahiti Village
**Luxury**
Four Seasons Las
  Vegas

## Center Strip

**Budget**
Bally's Las Vegas
Fairfield Inn Las Vegas
  Airport
Silver Sevens Hotel &
  Casino

**Mid-Range**
Alexis Park
Flamingo Las Vegas
The LINQ Hotel &
  Casino
Palms Casino Resort
Platinum Hotel
Rio All-Suite Hotel
  & Casino
Treasure Island (TI)
**Luxury**
Aria
Bellagio
Caesars Palace
The Cosmopolitan of
  Las Vegas
The Palazzo
The Venetian

## North Strip

**Budget**
Circus Circus
Lucky Dragon
Royal Resort

Shalimar Hotel
**Mid-Range**
Courtyard Las Vegas
  Convention Center
SLS Las Vegas
**Luxury**
Renaissance Las
  Vegas Hotel
Westgate Las Vegas
  Resort
Wynn Las Vegas

## Downtown

**Budget**
Main Street Station

## Farther Afield

**Budget**
Eastside Cannery
  Casino & Hotel
Hawthorn Suites by
  Wyndham Las
  Vegas/Henderson

# Sleeping A–Z

**PRICES**

Prices are approximate and
based on a double room for
one night.

| | |
|---|---|
| $$$ | over $200 |
| $$ | $120–$200 |
| $ | under $120 |

## ALEXIS PARK $$

alexispark.com
If you prefer to stay off The Strip
(▷ 155, panel), this small all-suite
hotel has 495 rooms, including
some fantastic two-level suites at a
really good price. It's also fairly
quiet and restful here. Facilities
include a hot tub and three pools.
The hotel provide guests with free
transport to and from The Strip.
✚ E9  ✉ 375 East Harmon Avenue
☎ 702/796-3300  🚌 108

## ARIA $$$

aria.com
Aria is the flagship hotel of the
stunning CityCenter complex
(▷ 18–19). The rooms and suites
have floor-to-ceiling windows to
match the glass-walled tower's
smooth lines, and guests enjoy
top-of-the-range gourmet dining
and nightlife.
✚ C10  ✉ 3730 Las Vegas Boulevard
South  ☎ 702/590-7757  🚌 Deuce

### BALLY'S LAS VEGAS $$$

ballyslasvegas.com

Bally's is the place to come for some "me time." The 2,549 rooms and 265 suites are spacious, with grand sitting areas and opulent bathrooms. There are floodlit tennis courts.

➕ D9 ✉ 3645 Las Vegas Boulevard South ☎ 702/739-4111 🚇 Bally's/Paris 🚌 Deuce

### BELLAGIO (▷ 14) $$$

bellagio.com

This is one of the most beautiful hotels in Vegas, built in the style of a huge Mediterranean villa with lovely gardens. The 3,950 rooms and suites are large and classy, and decorated in modern tones.

➕ C9–D9 ✉ 3600 Las Vegas Boulevard South ☎ 702/693-7111 🚌 Deuce, SDX

### CAESARS PALACE (▷ 16) $$$

caesarspalace.com

Ancient Rome prevails through classical temples, marble columns and every possible excess you can imagine. All 3,348 rooms and suites are luxurious, but even more so in the Octavius and Augustus towers, which have huge whirlpool tubs in the bathrooms.

➕ C8–D9 ✉ 3570 Las Vegas Boulevard South ☎ 702/731-7110 🚇 Flamingo/Caesars Palace 🚌 Deuce

### CIRCUS CIRCUS $

circuscircus.com

Although it is one of the oldest hotels on The Strip, Circus Circus still provides one of the best value-for-money options for families. It has nearly 3,800 seviceable rooms and suites.

➕ E6 ✉ 2880 Las Vegas Boulevard South ☎ 702/734-0410 🚌 Deuce

### THE COSMOPOLITAN OF LAS VEGAS (▷ 20) $$$

cosmopolitanlasvegas.com

The sheer-sided tower of The Cosmopolitan, next door to the happening CityCenter (▷ 18–19),

*The Flamingo is a good choice if you want to be close to the action*

offers nearly 3,000 rooms, studios and suites, some with balconies (a rarity on The Strip) or kitchenette. Cosmo's central showpiece is an amazing multistory chandelier, concealing three bars.

🚇 D9 ✉ 3708 Las Vegas Boulevard South ☎ 702/698-7000 🚌 Deuce

### COURTYARD LAS VEGAS CONVENTION CENTER $$

courtyard.marriott.com
Part of the well-known chain, this business hotel provides 149 better-than-average motel rooms (including 12 suites), plus a fitness center and an outdoor pool. It's located opposite the Las Vegas Convention Center, which has a monorail station.

🚇 F7 ✉ 3275 Paradise Road ☎ 702/791-3600 🚆 Las Vegas Convention Center 🚌 SDX

### DOUBLETREE BY HILTON $$$

lasvegasairportclub.doubletree.com
This plain concrete block is just 10 minutes from the airport, but is surprisingly quiet, and handy for late arrivals or early departures. The excellent value rooms have all mod-cons and free internet. There are regular free shuttles to the airport and to The Strip.

🚇 Off map ✉ 7250 Pollock Drive ☎ 702/948-4000 🚌 217

### EASTSIDE CANNERY CASINO & HOTEL $

eastsidecannery.com
Only 7 miles (11km) east of The Strip, this is a good-value option if you're going to Hoover Dam and the Grand Canyon. It has comfy rooms, a pool and hot tub.

🚇 Off map ✉ 5255 Boulder Highway ☎ 702/856-5300 🚌 202, BHX

### EXCALIBUR $

excalibur.com
Kids love this medieval castle with its moat and drawbridge. Parents might find it all just a little tacky, but it's probably one of the cheapest hotels on The Strip, and has more than 4,000 rooms and suites.

🚇 D10 ✉ 3850 Las Vegas Boulevard South ☎ 702/597-7777 🚌 Deuce, SDX

### FAIRFIELD INN LAS VEGAS AIRPORT $

fairfield.marriott.com
About a mile east of The Strip, this pristine, small hotel has a contemporary design. The 142 rooms are decorated in cheerful hues. Start your day with a complimentary hot breakfast buffet. There's a small outdoor pool and a fitness center.

🚇 F8 ✉ 3850 Paradise Road ☎ 702/791-0899 🚌 108

### FLAMINGO LAS VEGAS $$

caesars.com/flamingo-las-vegas
Bugsy Siegel's original 1946 Flamingo was rebuilt by the Hilton group in 1993. There are 3,565 units; the executive king rooms are spacious. It also has one of the best pool areas on The Strip.

**SLEEP**

155

➕ D9 ✉ 3555 Las Vegas Boulevard South ☎ 702/733-3111 🚌 Deuce

## FOUR SEASONS LAS VEGAS $$$

fourseasons.com

This hotel takes up the top five levels of Mandalay Bay (▷ 157), but retains its own tranquil identity. The 424 rooms and suites are elegantly decorated, and all the Mandalay Bay facilities are available to guests.

➕ D11 ✉ 3960 Las Vegas Boulevard South ☎ 702/632-5000 🚌 Flamingo/Caesars Palace 🚌 Deuce, SDX

## HAWTHORN SUITES BY WYNDHAM LAS VEGAS/HENDERSON $

wyndhamhotels.com

Hawthorn Suites is not too far off the beaten track. It's a good choice for families; the 71 suites are plain but some have kitchenettes and a balcony, and lots of extras. There is an indoor pool and fitness center.

➕ Off map ✉ 910 South Boulder Highway, Henderson ☎ 702/568-7800 🚌 217, BHX, HDX

## THE LINQ HOTEL & CASINO $$

caesars.com/linq

Right in the middle of the Strip, this casino hotel (formerly the Quad) has 2,600-plus rooms, all freshly renovated with a modern look. It's steps from the High Roller wheel and LINQ promenade.

➕ D8-D9 ✉ 3535 Las Vegas Boulevard South ☎ 702/322-0560 🚌 Harrah's/The LINQ 🚌 Deuce

## LUCKY DRAGON $

luckydragonlv.com

Opened in 2016, this Chinese-themed hotel holds more than 200 plush rooms with vermilion red accents, as well as Asian restaurants and an octagonal casino where a 1.25-ton glass dragon sculpture hangs suspended over the gaming tables.

➕ E6 ✉ 300 West Sahara Avenue ☎ 702/889-8018 🚌 Deuce, SDX

## LUXOR (▷ 30) $$

luxor.com

The 4,400-room Luxor may have moved away from its original Egyptian theme but you still enter beneath a huge sphinx and are transported to some hotel rooms via an elevator that travels up the slope of the pyramid.

➕ C11-D11 ✉ 3900 Las Vegas Boulevard South ☎ 702/262-4444 🚌 Deuce

## MAIN STREET STATION $

mainstreetcasino.com

This characterful hotel has a Victorian theme, with genuine

SLEEP

antiques, chandeliers, flickering gas lamps, iron railings and stained-glass windows. It has 406 bright rooms and a brewery.
⊞ G2 ✉ 200 North Main Street ☎ 702/387-1896 🚌 SDX

## MANDALAY BAY $$

mandalaybay.com
There is masses of big-city style at the Mandalay Bay. It's the only hotel in Las Vegas with a beach and a gigantic wave pool. There are 3,200-plus rooms and suites; even the standard rooms are huge, and all are light and airy.
⊞ C11–D11 ✉ 3950 Las Vegas Boulevard South ☎ 702/632-7777 🚌 Deuce, SDX

## MGM GRAND (▷ 34) $$

mgmgrand.com
This is pure Hollywood, with figures of famous stars dotted around the lobby and huge stills from classic movies on the walls. The 5,000-plus rooms offer a range of options, from the health-conscious "Stay Well" rooms to large spacious Strip-view suites.
⊞ D10 ✉ 3799 Las Vegas Boulevard South ☎ 702/891-1111 🚇 MGM Grand 🚌 Deuce, SDX

## MONTE CARLO $$

montecarlo.com
A popular choice for value-conscious visitors, the Monte Carlo has around 3,000 attractive rooms and suites.
⊞ D10 ✉ 3770 Las Vegas Boulevard South ☎ 702/730-7777 🚌 Deuce

## NEW YORK NEW YORK (▷ 44) $$

newyorknewyork.com
Staying in this huge mock-up of the New York City skyline is quite

an experience. The 2,000-plus rooms and suites are in a sophisticated style, decorated in earth tones and pastels. Light sleepers should request a room away from the Big Apple Coaster that thunders around outside.
⊞ D10 ✉ 3790 Las Vegas Boulevard South ☎ 702/740-6969 🚇 MGM Grand 🚌 Deuce

## THE PALAZZO $$

palazzo.com
Palazzo is a magnificent all-suite sister hotel to The Venetian (▷ 58–59), with similar Italian-style decor. The superb suites have fantastic views from higher floors. The pool deck has two seasonal day clubs, Azure and Tao Beach.
⊞ D8 ✉ 3355 Las Vegas Boulevard South ☎ 702/607-7777 🚌 Deuce

## PALMS CASINO RESORT $$

palms.com
As the name suggests, expect plenty of tropical foliage at this towering hotel. The Palms' reputation is due mainly to the clientele attracted to its nighttime haunts, such as the Ghostbar

---

### HOTEL TIPPING

As in any US city, it is customary to offer a gratuity to hotel employees for prompt and courteous service. Las Vegas has a huge number of different staff who provide such services, and who gets what can be confusing. The amount is at the customer's discretion but here are some general guidelines: bell captains and bellhops $2–$3 per bag; hotel maids $3 per day; valets $2–$3; use of concierge or VIP services $5–$20; restaurant servers 18 to 20 percent of the bill.

($\triangleright$ 130), which is located on the 55th floor. The 700 sleek rooms offer comfortable acccomodations, while the penthouse villas offer over-the-top luxury.

🔳 A9–B9 ✉ 4321 West Flamingo Road ☎ 702/942-7777 🚌 202

### PLATINUM HOTEL $$

theplatinumhotel.com

This non-gaming, smoke-free retreat is in urban contemporary style. The enormous 255 one- and two-bedroom suites each have a kitchen, a whirlpool tub and a balcony overlooking The Strip or the mountains. Make use of the soothing spa or indoor and outdoor pools.

🔳 E9 ✉ 211 East Flamingo Road ☎ 702/365-5000 🚌 202

### RENAISSANCE LAS VEGAS HOTEL $$$

renaissancelasvegas.com

For a retreat from the Vegas clamor and commotion, the Renaissance has cool and confident style without a slot machine in sight. The 578 rooms and suites are richly decorated and have a calming effect. There's also a swimming pool, hot tub, fitness center and an upscale steakhouse restaurant.

🔳 F7 ✉ 3400 Paradise Road ☎ 702/784-5700 🚌 108

### RIO ALL-SUITE HOTEL & CASINO $$

caesars.com/rio-las-vegas

This lively hotel in an off-Strip location offers great entertainment, a rooftop zip-line and two excellent buffets among its dining options. It has 2,548 huge, comfortable suites, with superb views from the floor-to-ceiling windows. There's free shuttle buses to The Strip for guests.

🔳 B8–B9 ✉ 3700 West Flamingo Road ☎ 702/777-7777 🚌 202

### ROYAL RESORT $

royalhotelvegas.com

The quiet non-casino Royal Resort is just off The Strip and offers good value for money. It has small but comfortable rooms; those at the front have a private balcony. Other amenities include a restaurant, cocktail bar, outdoor pool and gym.

🔳 E7 ✉ 199 Convention Center Drive ☎ 702/735-6117 🚌 Deuce

### SHALIMAR HOTEL $$

hojo.com

This low-rise motel is in a fair location north of The Strip and closer to Downtown. Some of the 100 rooms look out on the on-site wedding chapel. The motel's Florida Café offers Cuban cuisine.

🔳 F4 ✉ 1401 Las Vegas Boulevard South ☎ 702/388-0301 🚌 Deuce

### SILVER SEVENS HOTEL & CASINO $

silversevenscasino.com

Formerly Terrible's, this recently renovated hotel is anything but. It has smartly furnished rooms, a pool, hot tub and a 24-hour café, all at very agreeable rates.

🔳 F9 ✉ 4100 Paradise Road ☎ 702/733-7000 🚌 108

### SLS LAS VEGAS $$

slshotels.com/lasvegas

Flowering from the ashes of the vintage Sahara casino, this luxury hotel brand from LA offers up-to-the-minute styling in its 1,600 rooms and more than a dozen nightspots, boutique shops and restaurants.

🔳 E6–F6 ✉ 2535 Las Vegas Boulevard South ☎ 702/761-7000 🏨 SLS Las Vegas 🚌 Deuce, SDX

## TAHITI VILLAGE $$

tahitivillage.com

South of The Strip, this non-gaming resort features 300 one- or two-bedroom suites, equipped with either a full kitchen or kitchenette. Guests have use of a lagoon-style pool and free shuttles to The Strip and Downtown.

🔳 Off map ✉ 7200 Las Vegas Boulevard South ☎ 702/623-2746 🚌 SDX

## TREASURE ISLAND (TI) $$

treasureisland.com

This hotel has left behind its *Pirates of the Caribbean* swashbuckling image of the past for a more sophisticated adult take on the high seas. The nearly 3,000 rooms and suites, all renovated in contemporary style, have floor-to-ceiling windows.

🔳 D8 ✉ 3300 Las Vegas Boulevard South ☎ 702/894-7111 🚌 Deuce

## THE VENETIAN (▷ 58) $$$

venetian.com

Famous for its Italianate canals and replica of St. Mark's Square, The Venetian has more than 4,000 all-suite rooms. The decor varies, although all have marble bathrooms and fine furnishings. There are also excellent dining and shopping opportunities here and next door at The Palazzo, its sister resort.

🔳 D8 ✉ 3355 Las Vegas Boulevard South ☎ 702/414-1000 🚌 Deuce

---

### HOTEL GRADING

US hotels, including those in Las Vegas, are classified by the American Automobile Association (AAA, or Triple A) into five categories, from one to five diamonds. As this is based entirely on facilities offered, it does mean that hotels with four diamonds can be equally as luxurious as those with five, or that an attractively furnished atmospheric two-diamond bed-and-breakfast may cost less than a down-at-heel three-diamond business style hotel.

---

## WESTGATE LAS VEGAS RESORT $$$

westgatedestinations.com

Completely renovated in 2016, the former Las Vegas Hilton still offers fine accommodations in its nearly 3,000 guest rooms, each in an individual opulent style. Elvis revived his career here in 1969 (note the bronze statue of The King in the lobby), and the hotel was used in the Bond movie *Diamonds are Forever*.

🔳 F6 ✉ 3000 Paradise Road ☎ 702/732-5111 🏨 Las Vegas Convention Center 🚌 108

## WYNN LAS VEGAS (▷ 62) $$$

wynnlasvegas.com

Steve Wynn's latest incredible casino resort is one of the city's most lavish hotels, occupying almost 50 floors. The 2,700-plus rooms are huge, very stylish, and equipped with every luxury. There is an artificial lake and mountain and an 18-hole golf course.

🔳 D7–E7 ✉ 3131 Las Vegas Boulevard South ☎ 702/770-7000 🚌 Deuce, SDX

# Need to Know

**This section takes you through all the practical aspects of your trip to make it run more smoothly and to give you confidence before you go and while you are there.**

**NEED TO KNOW**

# Planning Ahead

## WHEN TO GO

With so many of its attractions under cover and not dependent on weather conditions, there's no off-season to speak of in Las Vegas. Avoid high summer if you don't like excessively hot weather, unless you plan to stay indoors.

| TIME |
| --- |
| Vegas is on Pacific Standard Time (GMT −8), advanced one hour between mid-March and November. |

### TEMPERATURE

| JAN | FEB | MAR | APR | MAY | JUN | JUL | AUG | SEP | OCT | NOV | DEC |
| --- | --- | --- | --- | --- | --- | --- | --- | --- | --- | --- | --- |
| 56°F | 62°F | 68°F | 78°F | 88°F | 98°F | 104°F | 102°F | 94°F | 81°F | 66°F | 57°F |
| 13°C | 17°C | 20°C | 25°C | 31°C | 36°C | 40°C | 39°C | 34°C | 27°C | 19°C | 14°C |

**Summer** (June to September) can be incredibly hot and oppressive, with daytime temperatures sometimes soaring as high as 120°F (49°C).

**Spring and autumn** are much more comfortable, with average temperatures usually reaching 70°F (21°C).

**Winter** (December to February) sees average temperatures above 50°F (10°C). There can be the odd chilly or rainy day when you will need a jacket and an umbrella, and sometimes it can drop below freezing at night.

### WHAT'S ON

**March** *NASCAR Weekend* (mid-Mar): A major event on the racing calendar, held at the Las Vegas Motor Speedway.

*St. Patrick's Day Parade* (Mar 17): A pub crawl Downtown kicks off other entertainment; Celtic bands, storytellers and dancers.

**April** *Vegas Uncork'd*: The city's premier food and wine festival brings foodies, chefs and sommeliers to The Strip.

**May** *Helldorado Days*: A Downtown parade, rodeo events and country-and-western festival celebrate the city's frontier days.

*Billboard Music Awards*: Music celebrities gather at the T-Mobile to honor the world's best music.

**May/July** *World Series of Poker:* The world's best poker players compete for supremacy at the Rio.

**July** *Fourth of July:* US Independence Day festivities, with general jollity everywhere, including superb fireworks displays at major resorts.

**October/November** *Professional Bull Riders World Finals:* Five days of cowboy rodeo action at T-Mobile Arena.

**November** *Rock 'n' Roll Marathon & 1/2:* Wildly costumed runners race past live bands on the neon-lit Strip.

**December** *National Finals Rodeo* (early Dec): During the 10-day finals, cowboys compete and Las Vegas goes country-mad, dressing up, line-dancing and barbecuing.

*New Year's Eve Celebrations:* A huge party held along The Strip and Downtown on the Fremont Street Experience.

**First Friday** A huge arts and entertainment party takes place on the first Friday of each month in Downtown's 18b Arts District (✉ ffflv.org ⏱ 5–11pm).

## LAS VEGAS ONLINE

### lasvegas.com
The official website of Las Vegas Convention and Visitors Authority offers well-presented information on everything you need to know when planning your trip to Las Vegas.

### reviewjournal.com
For articles on local news, listings, events and other sources of information, try this useful site run by the respected *Las Vegas Review Journal*, Nevada's largest newspaper.

### vegas.com
A comprehensive guide to hotels, entertainment, nightlife, events, attractions, activities and tours; offers online booking.

### vegasclick.com
This no-frills but information-packed site gives you tips about the Vegas casinos and the various games, plus lots of useful advice for visitors.

### lasvegasgolf.com
This site has detailed reviews on all the courses open in and around Las Vegas to help you plan a golfing holiday, and decide which courses you want to play.

### vegasexperience.com
This lively site is dedicated to the Fremont Street Experience. See what's going on at any time of the year, look for places to stay and find more things to do Downtown.

### gaylasvegas.com
The most complete site for GBLT locals and visitors to Las Vegas. It keeps up with the latest information on clubs, bars, restaurants and organizations, plus lots more.

### cheapovegas.com
Geared to the visitor who wants to do Vegas on a budget, this fun guide provides comprehensive reviews and unbiased opinions with a humorous slant.

## USEFUL WEBSITES

**rtcsnv.com/transit/**
Official site for the Regional Transportation Commission of Southern Nevada (RTC), the company responsible for the Las Vegas bus system. Use the transit system map, routes and schedule pages to discover exactly how to get from A to B.

**fodors.com**
A complete travel-planning site where you can research prices and weather; book air tickets, cars and rooms; pose questions (and get answers) to fellow visitors; and find links to other sites.

## INTERNET ACCESS

Most hotels in Las Vegas have business centers and offer internet access to their guests, but you have to be aware that most hotels charge for internet access (around $10–$20 per day), and for WiFi connection when using your own laptop. It is possible to find free access in some hotels, but usually only if the hotel already charges a mandatory nightly resort fee.

**NEED TO KNOW**

# Getting There

## ENTRY REQUIREMENTS

Visitors to the US must show a full passport, valid for at least six months. You must complete an Electronic System of Travel Authorization (ESTA™) before traveling to the USA. ESTA™ is a web-based system and can only be accessed online. For more information, and to complete the form, visit https://esta.cbp.dhs.gov. Most UK citizens and visitors from other countries belonging to the Visa Waiver Program can enter without a visa, but must have a return or onward ticket. Allow extra time for security checks. Regulations can change, so check before you travel with the US Embassy (☎ 020 7499 9000; uk.usembassy.gov).

## AIRPORT FACTS

● McCarran airport has two well-organized terminals with many shops, restaurants and snack bars.
● The airport underwent a $500 million expansion, with a new terminal, in 2012.
● 45 million passengers per year pass through the airport.
● It is the 26th busiest airport in the world.
● It is one of a few airports where you can play the slot machines while waiting for your luggage.

## AIRPORT

McCarran International Airport (LAS) is served by direct flights from cities right across North America, and there are intercontinental flights from London, Frankfurt and Tokyo. It is worth checking for special deals from airline and flight brokers, in newspapers and on the internet.

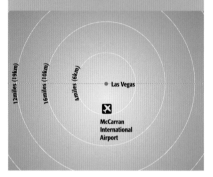

12 miles (19km)  16 miles (10km)  4 miles (6km)  ● Las Vegas

McCarran International Airport

### FROM MCCARRAN INTERNATIONAL AIRPORT

McCarran airport (tel 702/261-5211, mccarran.com) is 4 miles (6km) southeast of The Strip, at 5757 Wayne Newton Boulevard. Shuttles (including to McCarran Rent-a-Car Center), taxis and limousines pick up outside the terminals, and there are information desks throughout the airport.

Several companies run airport shuttle buses every 10 or 15 minutes from outside the baggage claim area—leave through door exits 7–13—and on Level Zero at Terminal 3. They all cost roughly the same (around $10 to The Strip or Downtown) and normally operate 24 hours. Most stop at all the major hotels and motels. No advance reservation required. Check first, as your resort hotel might offer an airport shuttle. Less expensive are the RTC buses (from $2 one way) that operate from outside the airport terminal: the Westcliff Airport Express (WAX) bus stops at the corner of Tropicana Ave and Las Vegas Blvd, where you can transfer to the Deuce (▷ 166), which stops close to most hotels along The Strip, or the faster Strip & Downtown Express (SDX) bus (▷ 166), which makes limited stops.

Taxis are easily available outside baggage claim at Terminal 1 and Level Zero at Terminal 3, and cost around $25 to the center of The Strip, or $35 to Downtown hotels (depends on traffic and destination). Stretch limos line up outside the airport waiting to take you to your destination; if you are tempted, try to share as they can be costly ($60 up to $115 per hour, depending on the size). Try Presidential Limousines (tel 702/438-5466) or Las Vegas Limousines (tel 702/888-4848). For car rentals, all major car rental companies are located off-site (▷ panel). There are buses and shuttles available to take you to the McCarran Rent-a-Car Center, about 3 miles (5km) from the terminals. It is better to reserve a car in advance.

### ARRIVING BY BUS

Greyhound (tel 800/231-2222, greyhound. com) operates services to Las Vegas from cities and towns in California and Nevada. Tickets can be purchased just prior to departure. This is a convenient and inexpensive way to travel, although not the most comfortable. All Greyhound buses arrive at Downtown's bus terminal at 200 South Main Street (tel 702/384-9561).

### ARRIVING BY CAR

Interstate 15 from Los Angeles to Vegas takes you through some of the most breathtaking scenery of the Mojave Desert. The journey takes 4–5 hours depending on road, weather and traffic conditions (delays are often caused by construction work). Carry plenty of water and a spare tire, and watch your fuel level.

### ARRIVING BY RAIL

Amtrak (tel 800/872-7245, amtrak.com), the national train company, does not offer a direct service to Las Vegas from Los Angeles. You can connect to the city by bus from other rail destinations in California and Arizona. There has been talk of a new high-speed rail line from Los Angeles to Las Vegas, but at the time of writing nothing had materialized.

---

### CAR RENTAL

Hotel information desks can advise about renting a car. Some companies will deliver to hotels and pick up at the end of the rental period.

| | |
|---|---|
| **Avis** | 702/531-1500 |
| **Budget** | 702/736-1212 |
| **Enterprise** | 702/795-8842 |
| **Hertz** | 702/262-7700 |
| **National** | 702/263-8411 |
| **Thrifty** | 702/896-7600 |

The airport's off-site McCarran Rent-a-Car Center is serviced by all the major rental companies. All customers will be transported to their vehicles by free shuttles. For information, call 702/261-6001.

---

### CUSTOMS

● Visitors from outside the US, aged 21 or over, may import duty-free: 200 cigarettes, or 100 cigars, or 2kg of tobacco; 1 liter of alcohol; and gifts up to $100 in value.

● Imports of wildlife souvenirs sourced from rare or endangered species may be illegal or require a special permit. Check your home country's customs rules.

● Restricted import items include meat, seeds, plants and fruit.

● Some medication bought over the counter abroad may be prescription-only in the US and could be confiscated. Bring a doctor's certificate for essential medication.

# Getting Around

## VISITORS WITH DISABILITIES

If you are a wheelchair user, on arrival at the airport you will find shuttle buses with wheelchair lifts to get you into the city. You will also find easy access to most restaurants, showrooms and lounges. All the hotel casinos have accessible slot machines, and many provide access to table games. Assisted listening devices are widely available. If you plan to rent a car, you can request a temporary disabled parking permit ($8.25–$13.15), which can be used throughout Nevada; contact the Nevada Department of Motor Vehicles (☎ 486-4386, dmvnv.com).

## WALKING

The Strip is 4 miles (6km) long, and it's a taxing walk in the heat. Wear comfortable shoes, sunglasses and sunscreen. Even if you use The Strip's transportation, you will still have to walk considerable distances to and from hotels and attractions. Overhead walkways and trams connect several places along The Strip. Make a note of the cross streets that punctuate The Strip to help get your bearings; some are named after the hotels along them.

Most of what you will want to see and do in Las Vegas is found along Las Vegas Boulevard South, which is well served by buses. The boulevard is divided into two parts: Downtown, between Charleston Boulevard and Washington Avenue; and The Strip, comprising several long blocks— Sahara, Spring Mountain, Flamingo, and Tropicana avenues. In 2004, the first leg of a multimillion dollar monorail was launched, providing a welcome addition to the options for getting up and down The Strip.

### BUSES
The RTC (Regional Transportation Commission of Southern Nevada (▷ 163), tel 702/228-7433), runs 55 bus routes throughout the entire system, some of which operate 24 hours a day. South Strip Transfer Terminal (SSTT) at Gillespie Street is a major transfer point. The Deuce provides transportation along The Strip between the SSTT and Downtown, with many stops along the way, and runs about every 15 minutes (during peak times), 24 hours a day. This double-decker bus accommodates 97 people. The faster Strip & Downtown Express (SDX) bus follows nearly the same route, making limited stops along Las Vegas Boulevard. The fare is $6 one-way or $8 for a day pass, which you can purchase on the bus or from vending machines (you need to have the exact fare because drivers can't give change). You can get a transfer from the driver for off-Strip destinations, so you don't have to pay again. Off-strip buses otherwise cost $2 one-way.

### DRIVING
Almost every hotel on Las Vegas Boulevard South has its own self-parking garage. The best way into these garages, avoiding the gridlock on The Strip, is via the back entrances. Valet parking is also available at the front (and sometimes other) entrances. The standard tip for valets is $2–$3 when they return your keys. The best advice about driving in Las Vegas is don't do it unless you have to. The

speed limit on The Strip is 30mph (48kph) north of Tropicana Avenue, 45mph (72kph) south of Tropicana Avenue. The wearing of seat belts is compulsory.

## MONORAILS
The monorail (tel 702/699-8222, lvmonorail. com) opened in 2004. Running from MGM Grand to SLS, it operates every day from 7am to 2am (Fri–Sun until 3am, Monday until midnight). It will take you from one end of The Strip to the other in just 15 minutes. There are seven stations: MGM Grand, Bally's/Paris, Flamingo/Caesars, Harrah's/The LINQ, Las Vegas Convention Center, Westgate Las Vegas and SLS Las Vegas. A single fare costs $5, an unlimited one-day pass is $12 and an unlimited three-day pass costs $28. There are a number of smaller free tram services courtesy of the hotels, including one between the Bellagio, CityCenter and Monte Carlo (every 15 minutes, 8am–4am), one between the Mandalay Bay, the Excalibur and the Luxor (every 3–7 minutes, 9am–10.30pm), and one between the Mirage and Treasure Island (every 5–15 minutes, 7am–2am).

## TAXIS AND LIMOUSINES
Taxis line up outside every hotel and can be called from your room. When out, you need to call or go to a cab stand; taxis can't be hailed in the street. Taxi drivers are familiar with all the shows and attractions, and can often offer a review and make recommendations. Remember to give more of a tip than the standard 10–15 percent of the fare. Give a bigger tip if they help with the door and your luggage. There are plenty of limousine services, which start at $45 ($55 for a stretch limo) per hour. Your hotel concierge can make the necessary arrangements.
Suggested taxi companies:
- ACE Cab Co. 702/888-4888
- Yellow Checker Star 702/873-8012
- Western Cab Co. 702/736-8000
- Presidential Limousine 702/438-5466

### ORGANIZED SIGHTSEEING

There is no shortage of Vegas-based tour companies offering trips from Vegas to wherever you want to go, but there are also plenty showing the best of the city sights. These tours can give you an insider's view on city attractions, along with a good overview and orientation, before you start exploring independently. Nearly every hotel in Las Vegas has a sightseeing desk from where you can book tours. If the tour bus approach doesn't appeal to you, there are all kinds of other options, including small-scale specialized tours with your own group of family or friends, or using a limousine to whisk you from place to place. Perhaps best of all, you can take to the skies in a helicopter for a bird's-eye view of the fantastic architecture and, on after-dark flights, the glittering lights. Reputable tour companies include Scenic Airlines (scenic.com), Pink Jeep Tours (pinkjeeptours.com) and Maverick Helicopters (maverickhelicopter.com) and Gray Line Tours (graylinelasvegas.com).

# Essential Facts

## MEDICAL TREATMENT

In medical emergencies call ☎ 911 or go to the emergency department of the nearest hospital. Emergency Room services are available 24 hours at University Medical Center (✉ 1800 West Charleston Boulevard ☎ 702/383-2000), or Sunrise Hospital and Medical Center (✉ 3186 South Maryland Parkway ☎ 702/731-8000). Pharmacy telephone numbers are listed under "Pharmacies" or "Drugstores" in the Yellow Pages. 24-hour and night pharmacies are available at Walgreens (✉ 3339 Las Vegas Boulevard South ☎ 702/369-8166), and at CVS (✉ 3758 Las Vegas Boulevard South ☎ 702/262-9284).

## ELECTRICITY

Voltage is 110/120 volts AC (60 cycles) and sockets take two-prong, flat-pin plugs or three-pronged plugs with an additional rounded ground. European appliances also need a voltage transformer.

## EMERGENCY NUMBERS

Police: 911
Fire: 911
Ambulance: 911
American Automobile Association (AAA) breakdown service: 800/222-4357.

## ETIQUETTE

● Tip staff at least 15–20 percent in a restaurant, taxi drivers 10–15 percent for a direct route, porters $2–$3 per bag, depending on the distance carried, and valet parking attendants $2–$3 when they return your car.

● Las Vegas is one of the few pro-smoking places left in the US. Most hotels have designated smoking rooms, but smoking isn't allowed inside shopping malls, restaurants or bars that serve food.

● Dress is very informal during the day, and shorts and T-shirts are generally accepted anywhere. In the evening, smart-casual is more the norm, and some lounges, night-clubs and restaurants may have a dress code.

## GAMING

Nevada law permits a wide variety of gaming, but the most popular games are roulette, blackjack, craps and slot machines. If you are new to the game, spend some time watching before actually taking the plunge; you could pick up a few tips from the hard-and-fast gamblers. Punters have to be 21 to play. Most casinos do not have windows or clocks, so you are unaware of time passing, and they will often keep you refueled with free drinks and snacks. One benefit of all this cash changing hands is that much of the gaming taxes collected by the state are funneled into public education.

## Glossary of terms:

**Action**  Gaming activity measured by the amount wagered.

**Bank**  The person covering the bets in any game, usually the casino.

**Buy-in**  Purchasing of chips.

**Cage**  The cashier's section of the casino.

**Even money**  Bet that pays off at one to one.

**House edge**  The mathematical advantage the casino enjoys on every game and wager.

**House odds**  The ratio at which the casino pays off a winning bet.

**Limit**  The minimum/maximum bet accepted.

**Loose machine**  A slot machine set to return a high percentage on the money you put in.

**Marker**  An IOU owed to the casino by someone playing on credit.

**Toke**  A tip or gratuity.

## LOST PROPERTY

● For property lost on public transportation: South Strip Transfer Terminal, South Gilespie Street, tel 702/676-1849; daily 6–10.

● For property lost at McCarran International Airport: tel 702/261-5134; daily 7.30–6.

● Report losses of passports or credit cards to the police.

## NATIONAL HOLIDAYS

Jan 1: New Year's Day
3rd Mon in Jan: Martin Luther King Jr. Day
3rd Mon in Feb: President's Day
Mar/Apr: Easter (public holiday Good Friday)
Last Mon in May: Memorial Day
Jul 4: Independence Day
1st Mon in Sep: Labor Day
2nd Mon in Oct: Columbus Day
Nov 11: Veterans Day
4th Thu in Nov: Thanksgiving
Dec 25: Christmas Day

## OPENING HOURS

● Casinos: 24 hours a day, 7 days a week.
● Banks: Mon–Fri 9–5 or later, and some Sat mornings and early afternoons.
● Post offices: normally Mon–Fri 9–5, with limited hours on Sat.

---

### MONEY

● Credit cards are widely accepted.
● Most banks have ATMs.
● US-dollar traveler's checks are accepted as cash in most places, but ID may be requested.
● Most major hotels will exchange foreign currency, and there are several exchange bureaus on The Strip. You can also change money at major banks.

### CURRENCY

The unit of currency is the dollar ($), divided into 100 cents. Bills (notes) are in denominations of $1, $5, $10, $20, $50 and $100. Coins are 1 cent (penny), 5 cents (nickel), 10 cents (dime), 25 cents (quarter) and 50 cents (half dollar).

## NEWSPAPERS AND MAGAZINES

● Las Vegas has two daily newspapers: the *Las Vegas Review-Journal* and the *Las Vegas Sun*.
● Free *Las Vegas Weekly* has club listings and restaurant and bar reviews.
● Freebie tourist mags with coupons include 24/7 and Las Vegas Magazine.

## TELEPHONES

There are public payphones in hotels, casinos, stores, restaurants, gas stations and on many street corners. Local calls from a phone booth cost around 50 cents. Some phones are equipped to take prepaid phone cards and/or credit cards. Dial 1 plus the area code for numbers within the United States and Canada (note that international rates apply for the latter). Calls made from hotel rooms are very expensive. Las Vegas' area code is 702, which does not need to be dialed if you are calling within the city. To call Las Vegas from the UK, dial 00 followed by 1 (the code for the US and Canada), then the number. To call the UK from Las Vegas, dial 00 44, then drop the first zero from the area code.

● Stores: usually open at 10am; closing times vary, and may be earlier or later on weekends.
● Museums: see individual entries for details.
● Las Vegas boasts that it never closes and never sleeps, but off-Strip stores and banks, and peripheral businesses, will be closed on Sundays on certain holidays.

### POST OFFICES

● Main post office: 1001 East Sunset Road, near the airport, tel 702/361-9200; Mon–Fri 8–9, Sat 8–4. There are many post offices in the city. You can also mail letters and parcels from your hotel.
● Buy stamps from shops and from machines.
● US mailboxes are blue.

### SENSIBLE PRECAUTIONS

Carry only as much money with you as you need; leave other cash and valuables in the hotel safe. At night, avoid hotel parking lots and always enter the hotel via the main entrance. Report theft or mugging on the street to the police department immediately. Make sure your room is locked when you leave. Locks can be changed regularly in hotels for security reasons. Keep a close eye on your chips when playing the casino tables as thefts have been reported.

### STUDENT TRAVELERS

Discounts are sometimes available to students who have an International Student Identity Card (ISIC).

### TOILETS

There is never a shortage of clean, free public restrooms to be found on The Strip and Downtown in hotels, casinos, restaurants and bars.

### TOURIST INFORMATION OFFICE

Las Vegas Visitor Information Center: 3150 Paradise Road, Las Vegas, NV 89109, tel 702/892-7575, visitlasvegas.com, open Mon–Fri 8–5.30.

# Books and Films

## BOOKS

*Fear and Loathing in Las Vegas* by Hunter S. Thompson (1971). Hallucinogenic, drug- and alcoholic-fueled misadventures of "gonzo" journalist Thompson and his deranged lawyer, covering a motorcycle race in Las Vegas. Made into a film (1998), starring Johnny Depp.

*Inside Las Vegas* by Mario Puzo (1977). Illustrated retrospective of vintage Vegas by *The Godfather* author, with grainy photos revealing the seamier side of life on The Strip.

*Literary Las Vegas: The Best Writing About America's Most Fabulous City* edited by Mike Tronnes (1995). Anthology of essays and short stories about Vegas mobsters, showgirls, millionaires and celebs, as well as weightier themes such as atomic bomb testing.

*When the Mob Ran Vegas* by Steve Fischer (2005). Subtitled "Stories of Money, Mayhem and Murder," which sums it up nicely. Gripping anecdotes and inside accounts of the colorful but scary characters who controlled Sin City in the 1950s and 1960s.

## FILMS

*Ocean's 11* (1960). Buddies behaving badly, starring Frank Sinatra, Dean Martin and Sammy Davis Jr., as 11 old friends planning to rob five Vegas casinos in one night. The remake trilogy, beginning with *Ocean's Eleven* (2001), also features an all-star cast. Look out for an all-female spin-off, *Ocean's Eight* in 2018.

*Rain Man* (1988). Conniving Charlie Babbitt (Tom Cruise) tries to dupe his autistic savant brother Raymond (Dustin Hoffman) into hitting the jackpot at Caesars Palace.

*Casino* (1995). Corrupt casino boss Sam Rothstein (Robert De Niro) looks on as his city transforms from mobster empire to family-friendly resort. A powerful Martin Scorsese epic, soaked in blood, power and greed.

*The Hangover* (2009) When everything that could go wrong during a stag party in Vegas does, raunchy hijinks ensue.

### SIN CITY

With its origins firmly rooted in vice, corruption and scandal, Las Vegas has always provided a rich source of material for novelists and screenwriters. The weird, the shocking and the extreme are everyday occurrences in real life, re-created in gangster thrillers, such as *Casino*; glitz musicals, like *Viva Las Vegas* starring Elvis Presley; and the escapist road-trip fantasy novel and film *Fear and Loathing in Las Vegas*. And as the ultimate dream of many visitors is to be the lucky one to defy the casino's odds and break the bank, Sin City is likely to be a source of inspiration for many years to come.

# Index

The Automobile Association would like to thank the following photographers, companies and picture libraries for their assistance in the preparation of this book.

2t AA/C Sawyer; 2ct Wynn Las Vegas/Barbara Kraft; 2c AA/C Sawyer; 2cb MGM Resorts International; 2b, 3t AA/C Sawyer; 3ct AA/L Dunmire; 3cb Kumar Sriskandan/Alamy Stock Photo; 4t AA/C Sawyer; 5 SV/Alamy Stock Photo; 6/7t AA/C Sawyer, 6r AA/C Sawyer; 6/7ct AA/C Sawyer; 6/7b Kobby Dagan/VWPics/Alamy Stock Photo; 7l AA/C Sawyer; 8/9t AA/L Dunmire; 8/9ctl Stratosphere Hotel/Marc Paulus; 8/9ctr Harrahs/courtesy of Caesars Palace Las Vegas; 8/9cbl AA/C Sawyer, 8/9cbr MGM Resorts International, 8/9b Caesars Entertainment; 10bl Getty Images; 10br Bloomberg/Getty Images; 11 Getty Images; 12 Neon Museum; 14 AA/C Sawyer; 14/5ct AA/L Dunmire; 14/5cb Mathew Allen; 15 AA/L Dunmire; 16 AA/Sawyer; 17ct, 17cb AA/C Sawyer; 17r Harrahs/courtesy of Caesars Palace Las Vegas; 18l MGM Resorts International; 18tr Jerry Ballard/Alamy Stock Photo; 18/9c Alun Reece/Alamy Stock Photo; 19l eye35.co.uk/Alamy Stock Photo; 19r Shirley Kilpatrick/Alamy Stock Photo; 20l, 20/21 David Giral/Alamy Stock Photo; 22 AA/C Sawyer; 23tl AA/C Sawyer; 23cl Sundlof – EDCO/Alamy Stock Photo; 23r, 24l, 24/25t AA/C Sawyer; 24/5b Robert Harding World Imagery/Alamy Stock Photo; 25, 26l, 27l, 27tr, 27cr AA/C Sawyer; 28 Caesars Entertainment; 28/9t Caesars Entertainment/Denise Truscello; 28/9b Caesars Entertainment/Denise Truscello; 29 Caesars Entertainment; 30 MGM Resorts International; 30/1t AA/L Dunmire; 30/1c, 31t, 31c MGM Resorts International; 32 Madame Tussauds; 33cr, 32/3c, 33c, 32/3t AA/C Sawyer; 36, 37tl, 37tr, 37c MGM Resorts International; 38/9 The Mob Museum; 39t The Mob Museum/John Gurzinski; 39c The Mob Museum/Jeff Green; 40 Courtesy of the Atomic Testing Museum, Las Vegas, Nevada, atomictestingmuseum.org; 40/1 Jeff Greenberg 6 of 6/Alamy Stock Photo; 42, 42/3, 43 Neon Museum; 44 MGM Resorts International; 44/45t, 45cr, 45tr, 45c, 46l, 46tr, 46/47c, 47tl, 47r AA/C Sawyer; 48tl, 48cl, 48/9 MGM Resorts International; 49cr AA/C Sawyer; 50l AA/L Dunmire; 50/51, 51r, 52, 53tl AA/C Sawyer; 53ct, 53cl, 53cr MGM Resorts International; 54l, 54/55, 55tr, 55br courtesy of The Smith Center; 56l, 56/57t AA/C Sawyer; 56cr Stratosphere Hotel; 57, 58tl, 58/59c, 59tl, 59tr, 59cr, 60l, 60/61, 61tl, 61tr AA/C Sawyer; 61c AA/L Dunmire; 62l, 62/33t AA/C Sawyer; 62cr John Warburton-Lee Photography/Alamy Stock Photo; 63cl AA/C Sawyer; 63cr Wynn Las Vegas; 64 Slotzilla; 66bl The Auto Collections, Las Vegas; 66br Canyon Ranch; 67bl, 67br, 68bl MGM Resorts International; 68br Four Seasons Hotel Spa; 69b, 70 AA/C Sawyer; 71bl Hollywood Cars Museum; 71br PCL/Alamy Stock Photo; 72bl Caesars Entertainment; 72br John Elk III/Alamy Stock Photo; 73bl Pole Position Raceway; 73br Slotzilla; 74bl AA/C Sawyer; 74br MGM Resorts International; 75 Niebrugge Images/Alamy Stock Photo; 76bl Tibor Bognar/Alamy Stock Photo; 76br Photodisc; 77bl, 77br, 78bl, 78br, 79bl, 79br AA/C Sawyer; 80 MGM Resorts International; 82t The Mob Museum/Jim Decker; 82c, 82b AA/C Sawyer; 83t, 83b MGM Resorts International; 86t AA/L Dunmire; 86ct MGM Resorts International; 86cb AA/C Sawyer; 86b Darrin Bush Las Vegas News Bureau, 88t, 88c AA/C Sawyer; 88b MGM Resorts International; 89t AA/C Sawyer; 89b AA/L Dunmire; 92br, 94t, 94b AA/C Sawyer; 95t Yaacov Dagan Alamy Stock Photo; 95b AA/C Sawyer; 98t Stratosphere Hotel; 98c, 98b AA/C Sawyer; 100cl The Mob Museum; 100cr PCL/Alamy Stock Photo; 101t Neon Museum; 101b, 104t, 104ct AA/C Sawyer; 104c The Mob Museum; 104cb Neon Museum; 104b courtesy of The Smith Center; 105 Slotzilla; 106c AA/M Van Vark; 106b, 107t AA/C Sawyer; 107b Getty Images; 110t, 110c, 111, 112, 114/115t, 114ct, 114cb, 114/115b, 115ct, 115cb AA/C Sawyer; 118 Richard Green/Alamy Stock Photo; 120, 123 AA/C Sawyer; 124 MGM Resorts International; 126/127t AA/C Sawyer; 126ct The Wynn/Tomasz & Rossa; 126cb MGM Resorts International, 126/127b, 127ct AA/C Sawyer; 127cb MGM Resorts International; 130 AA/C Sawyer; 133 Penn & Teller; 135 Aurora Photos/Alamy Stock Photo; 136 AA/C Sawyer; 138t ImageState; 138ct MGM Resorts International, 138cb AA/C Sawyer; 138b MGM Resorts International; 145 AA/C Sawyer; 148 Kumar Sriskandan/Alamy Stock Photo; 150 MGM Resorts International; 152t, 152c AA/C Sawyer; 152b MGM Resorts International; 154 AA/C Sawyer; 160 Kumar Sriskandan/Alamy Stock Photo.

Every effort has been made to trace the copyright holders, and we apologize in advance for any unintentional omissions or errors. We would be happy to apply any corrections in a following edition of this publication.

# Las Vegas 25 Best

**WRITTEN BY** Jackie Staddon and Hilary Weston
**ADDITIONAL WRITING BY** Huw Hennessy
**UPDATED BY** Sara Benson
**SERIES EDITOR** Clare Ashton
**COVER DESIGN** Chie Ushio, Yuko Inagaki
**DESIGN WORK** Liz Baldin
**IMAGE RETOUCHING AND REPRO** Ian Little

Published in the United Kingdom by AA Publishing

**ISBN 978-0-1475-4708-8**

**SIXTH EDITION**

All details in this book are based on information supplied to us at press time. Always confirm information when it matters, especially if you're making a detour to visit a specific place. Fodor's expressly disclaims any liability, loss, or risk, personal or otherwise, that is incurred as a consequence of the use of any of the contents of this book.

**SPECIAL SALES**
This book is available for special discounts for bulk purchases for sales promotions or premiums. For more information, email specialmarkets@penguinrandomhouse.com.

Color separation by AA Digital Department
Printed and bound by Leo Paper Products, China

10 9 8 7 6 5 4 3 2 1

A05522
Maps in this title produced from map data supplied by Global Mapping, Brackley, UK © Global Mapping and data from openstreetmap.org
© OpenStreetMap contributors
Transport maps © Communicarta Ltd, UK